HAUNTING JULIA

by Alan Ayckbourn

samuelfrench.co.uk

FOR AMATEUR PRODUCTION ENQUIRIES

UNITED KINGDOM AND WORLD
EXCLUDING NORTH AMERICA

plays@samuelfrench.co.uk

020 7255 4302/01

Each title is subject to availability from Samuel French, depending upon country of performance.

THINKING ABOUT PERFORMING A SHOW?

There are thousands of plays and musicals available to perform from Samuel French right now, and applying for a licence is easier and more affordable than you might think

From classic plays to brand new musicals, from monologues to epic dramas, there are shows for everyone.

Plays and musicals are protected by copyright law, so if you want to perform them, the first thing you'll need is a licence. This simple process helps support the playwright by ensuring they get paid for their work and means that you'll have the documents you need to stage the show in public.

Not all our shows are available to perform all the time, so it's important to check and apply for a licence before you start rehearsals or commit to doing the show.

LEARN MORE & FIND THOUSANDS OF SHOWS

Browse our full range of plays and musicals, and find out more about how to license a show
www.samuelfrench.co.uk/perform

Talk to the friendly experts in our Licensing team for advice on choosing a show and help with licensing
plays@samuelfrench.co.uk   020 7387 9373

Acting Editions

BORN TO PERFORM

Playscripts designed from the ground up to work the way you do in rehearsal, performance and study

---

Larger, clearer text for easier reading

Wider margins for notes

Performance features such as character and props lists, sound and lighting cues, and more

---

+ CHOOSE A SIZE AND STYLE TO SUIT YOU

 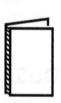 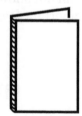

STANDARD EDITION

Our regular paperback book at our regular size

SPIRAL-BOUND EDITION

The same size as the Standard Edition, but with a sturdy, easy-to-fold, easy-to-hold spiral-bound spine

LARGE EDITION

A4 size and spiral bound, with larger text and a blank page for notes opposite every page of text – perfect for technical and directing use

---

| LEARN MORE | **samuelfrench.co.uk/actingeditions** |

Other plays by ALAN AYCKBOURN
published and licensed by Samuel French

Mixed Doubles

Mr. A's Amazing Maze Plays

Mr Whatnot

My Very Own Story

My Wonderful Day

Neighbourhood Watch

The Norman Conquests: Table Manners; Living Together;
Round and Round the Garden

Private Fears in Public Places

Relatively Speaking

The Revengers' Comedies

RolePlay

Roundelay

Season's Greetings

Sisterly Feelings

Snake in the Grass

Suburban Strains

Sugar Daddies

Taking Steps

Ten Times Table

Things We Do for Love

This Is Where We Came In

Time and Time Again

Time of My Life

Tons of Money (revised)

Way Upstream

Wildest Dreams

Wolf at the Door

Woman in Mind

A Word from Our Sponsor

**Other plays by ALAN AYCKBOURN
licensed by Samuel French**

The Boy Who Fell Into a Book

Invisible Friends

The Jollies

Orvin – Champion of Champions

Surprises

Whenever

**FIND PERFECT PLAYS TO PERFORM AT
www.samuelfrench.co.uk/perform**

ABOUT THE AUTHOR

Alan Ayckbourn has worked in theatre as a playwright and director for over fifty years, rarely if ever tempted by television or film, which perhaps explains why he continues to be so prolific. To date he has written more than eighty plays, many one act plays and a large amount of work for the younger audience. His work has been translated into over thirty-five languages, is performed on stage and television throughout the world and has won countless awards.

Major successes include: *Relatively Speaking, How the Other Half Loves, Absurd Person Singular, Bedroom Farce, A Chorus of Disapproval,* and *The Norman Conquests.* In recent years, there have been revivals of *Season's Greetings* and *A Small Family Business* at the National Theatre; in the West End *Absent Friends, A Chorus of Disapproval, Relatively Speaking* and *How the Other Half Loves*; and at Chichester Festival Theatre, major revivals of *Way Upstream* in 2015, and *The Norman Conquests* in 2017.

Artistic Director of the Stephen Joseph theatre from 1972–2009, where almost all his plays have been first staged, he continues to direct his latest new work there. He has been inducted into American Theater's Hall of Fame, received the 2010 Critics' Circle Award for Services to the Arts and became the first British playwright to receive both Olivier and Tony Special Lifetime Achievement Awards. He was knighted in 1997 for services to the theatre.

MUSIC USE NOTE

Licensees are solely responsible for obtaining formal written permission from copyright owners to use copyrighted music in the performance of this play and are strongly cautioned to do so. If no such permission is obtained by the licensee, then the licensee must use only original music that the licensee owns and controls. Licensees are solely responsible and liable for all music clearances and shall indemnify the copyright owners of the play(s) and their licensing agent, Samuel French, against any costs, expenses, losses and liabilities arising from the use of music by licensees. Please contact the appropriate music licensing authority in your territory for the rights to any incidental music.

IMPORTANT BILLING AND CREDIT REQUIREMENTS

If you have obtained performance rights to this title, please refer to your licensing agreement for important billing and credit requirements.

FIRST PERFORMANCE INFO

HAUNTING JULIA

The World premiere took place on 20 April 1994 at the Stephen Joseph Theatre, Scarborough

With the following cast:

JOE	Ian Hogg
ANDY	Damien Goodwin
KEN	Adrian McLoughlin
VOICE OF JULIA	Cathy Sara

Director: Alan Ayckbourn
Design: Jan Bee Brown
Lighting: Jackie Staines
Music: John Pattison

Stage Manager: Jane Eliot-Webb
Deputy Stage Manager: Jo Alexander
Assistant Stage Manager: Emma Gordon

CHARACTERS

JOE – a man in his sixties
ANDY – a man in his thirties
KEN – a man in his forties
JULIA – her voice

SETTING

A room in the Julia Lukin Music Centre

TIME

ACT I: One Sunday afternoon in November
ACT II: A moment earlier

AUTHOR'S NOTE

It is the author's preference that this play be presented in one act. However, appreciating that intervals are often deemed necessary for various reasons, if the play is to be presented in two acts, the interval should come at the point marked in the script.

ACT I

Sunday afternoon. 3.00 pm. November.

A room in the Julia Lukin Centre. The centre is one of those walk round 'living' experiences, created to commemorate historical people or past events either factual or fictional. In this case as a homage to a factual person. The room in question is a student's attic bedroom. Typical in many ways apart from an unnatural tidiness. From what we can see, we glean the following:

The occupant in question was a **WOMAN**, *though there are few obvious signs to indicate this. A neatly made bed with a clean white counterpane. An easy chair. Bookshelves. A chest of drawers, cupboard, etc. A small writing table upon which is some manuscript paper and pencils rather artistically laid out. A half finished mug of 'cocoa'. Bare boards with the occasional rug. Rather depressing wallpaper. One window looking out on to a back alley. Bleakly lit. A work room rather than a home, indicating someone with few or no personal items of sentimental value apart from one rather battered teddy bear on the bed.*

The door to the room itself is ajar, neither fully closed nor fully opened, it is all arranged to look as though the occupant has slipped out for a few moments but will return at any second. But for all this the overall impression is of a carefully arranged stage set dressed with an orderly clutter. In fact on the other side of the door is a solid brick wall. The original entrance to the room has been blocked off.

At the other end of the room from the door is a carpeted section cordoned off by some ornamental rope, forming a narrow corridor. This has been created by knocking down the adjoining wall through to the next door house. It is from here that the visitor to the centre is able to view the room, entering via a newly created archway.

In this section there is a free-standing pedestal fixed to the floor. Mounted on this is a large red button which, when pressed, operates the pre-recorded spoken commentary about the room.

At the start, **ANDY,** *a man in his early thirties is standing behind the ropes, staring at the room. He is in his street clothes which suggest that it's a cold day outside and a not much warmer one inside. Smart but not expensive clothes. He's made a bit of an effort.*

He stands for a long time without moving.

ANDY *(at length)* My God. *(He shakes his head)*

He presses the red button. Through the overhead speakers, a young **WOMAN**'s *voice is heard. He looks up, startled for a second, then listens.*

WOMAN Finally, this is the place where I spent most of my time while I was at college here. The house was then a student residence and this was my room when I was at the university, as a result of winning my music scholarship. It was a considerable change after my home in Otley, West Yorkshire, I can tell you. Quite modest, isn't it? I wonder what Mozart would have made of it! Amazing to think that it was at that small table which you can see there that I wrote over thirty of my hundred plus compositions including my three string quartets, an unfinished symphony for orchestra and solo wind instruments, and two of the three movements from my very popular Ridings Suite. All in pencil with not a piano in sight, mark you. Just me and Emily – that's my favourite teddy bear sitting on the bed there...

JOE, a man in his sixties, comes in through the archway.
He stops as he hears the commentary and stands listening
reverently. ANDY *becomes aware of him and makes to*
speak but JOE *holds up his hand and they continue to*
listen in silence.

I always preferred to work straight on to the manuscript,
often working till three or four o'clock in the morning while
the ideas were still fresh and buzzing around in my brain –
and besides, if you'd ever heard my piano playing you'd
know why. I lived here for nearly eighteen months, seeing
the occasional visitor or rushing off for lectures or a tutorial
but, in between, mostly just doing what I loved best of all,
sitting here with my head full of music, writing away for
dear life – I suppose that's what I lived for, really. My music.

A brief silence on the recording. Then: –.

MAN It was in this same room that on Tuesday, February 16th
1982, at the age of 19, Julia Lukin was found dead. The
victim of an overdose of alcohol and drugs – the tragic end
to a brief but brilliant life. We can only be thankful that
her music lives on after her...

A moment's silence.

JOE I wrote that.

ANDY Very good.

JOE With a bit of help. Done it well, haven't they?

ANDY It's really good. Quite moving. Very like her voice.

JOE Yes, well, get it right. Might as well get it right. They got
hold of this actress. I played her some home recordings.
She picked it up like that. Clever. She could do anyone.
Bette Davis, Meryl Streep, Mrs Thatcher... The firm that
did this – they use her all the time. They recommended
her... She's just done Boadicea for them... Big exhibition
near Colchester. She never stops apparently...

ANDY Who were the firm?

JOE *(vaguely)* Oh these – these people from – er... I forget
their name now. They're experts. They do masses of it.
They're doing it everywhere. Living experiences, interactive
exhibition centres, they're the thing these days, you know.

ANDY Oh, I know, yes. We –

JOE In my day, you know, we'd go to a museum, as kids, we'd
be expected just to stand there looking at the cases. If you
were lucky they sometimes gave you a handle you could
wind, make it move a bit but that was your lot. Nothing
more. Just shut up, keep moving and take your sticky fingers
off the glass. Blokes in blue peak caps, you know, clip you
round the ear soon as look at you just to pass the time. Not
nowadays. In some of these places these days, you know,
they practically jump out and talk to you personally. Well,
they do. In the States, you know, when Dolly and I went
last year – last holiday we had before she died – where was
it we went? – Montana, Alabama, I forget now – this Red
Indian Chief comes up – not a real one – turns round to
Dolly and starts talking to her. Hallo, paleface squaw and
so on. Gave Dolly a turn. He'd been standing that still till
then, you know, she thought he was stuffed. You know, like
a waxwork. Jumped out of her skin. *(He laughs)* So you
think it's alright? What I've done here?

ANDY I think it's great.

JOE I mean you don't think I've gone over? Sentimental, you
know?

ANDY No, not really.

JOE Only I know when we were planning it, you know, Dolly
said to me for God's sake, I know you, don't get sentimental.
You'll have them all crying before they're halfway round,
asking for their money back...

ANDY It's fine.

JOE I mean, I think it should be moving, I think it should
move you...

ANDY It does.

JOE So long as it's not sentimental.

ANDY It's not. Not at all.

JOE You reckon Dolly would have approved, then?

ANDY I'm sure she would.

JOE I only wish she'd lived to see it. This is Julia's very room, you know.

ANDY I know. I remember.

JOE The actual one. I bought this house and the two on either side. And then we knocked through there, you see. Just where we came in.

ANDY Yes, I see.

JOE To make a little – like – a viewing area.

ANDY Very effective.

JOE I mean we could have made the main entrance through her actual door as it used to be – that door there – but then I didn't think that would be so dramatic. Also we had a bit of bother with the safety officer at this level, up at attic level, it was apparently alright ten years ago for students to burn to death, but not your general public. But anyway, mostly, I wanted it to be dramatic.

ANDY Quite.

JOE They have to be dramatic, these things. Not, you know excessive, but dramatic. But this way, you see, I think – well, she could be coming through that door any time. Julia. Couldn't she?

ANDY Yes.

JOE Don't you think?

ANDY Oh, yes.

JOE You know the way it is, half open, half shut, in your mind's eye, you can practically see her, can't you...?

ANDY *(rather uneasily)* Yes.

JOE I can...

ANDY *(gently)* She's been dead twelve years, Joe.

JOE I don't need reminding.

ANDY She isn't going to come through that door, is she?

JOE No. She's not, I know. Anyway, it's solid brick the other side of that. We had to put a new wall in. Need a bulldozer to get in that way. Still, in your mind's eye...you know. You can't help imagining, can you?

ANDY Well.

Pause.

JOE Anyway. What do you make of the place? What you've seen?

ANDY *(tactfully)* I think you've done an amazing job. It's most impressive.

JOE Two rehearsal rooms, six practise rooms. A lecture theatre. Offices, canteen. Everything you want. The Julia Lukin Centre. Dream come true, this.

ANDY Yes.

JOE All done properly. Everything's acoustic, you know.

ANDY I could see that.

JOE I appreciate you coming over to see me today, I really do. You and Kay and the kids.

ANDY That's OK.

JOE Giving up your Sunday.

ANDY No problem. Delicious lunch...

JOE Sorry they couldn't all come along with us to have a look. But I wanted you to see it on your own. That didn't cause embarrassment, did it? Only I sensed a bit of awkwardness. I didn't mean to make it awkward between you and Kay.

ANDY *(awkwardly)* No, that was fine. As you saw, the kids are a bit snuffly, anyway – well, Simeon is. I think Naomi's over it now, at last. And I don't think Kay would really have wanted to come here, anyway.

JOE It wouldn't have upset her, would it? Coming over here?

ANDY Er...well, it might have. Just a little bit.

JOE Whatever for? You mean because of Julia?

ANDY Well...

JOE When you were with Julia, you didn't even know Kay, did you?

ANDY Barely, no.

JOE What do you mean, barely? Not at all you didn't.

ANDY No.

JOE Well then. How are you both, anyway? In yourselves? Alright?

ANDY Oh, yes.

JOE The youngsters are growing. Especially Naomi. Young woman now. Very nearly.

ANDY She's only eight.

JOE Ah well, these days. Don't mind me saying but Kay's looking a bit tired. I thought.

ANDY Yes?

JOE Bit drawn, you know. Sharp in her manner. Sharp with the kids. Don't let her get like that with them... No way to treat kids, shouting at them, you know...

ANDY No, well, she's not usually... I think they sometimes get a bit on her nerves – it's understandable – she's working very hard at the moment.

JOE I'm sorry, that's never an excuse. In my book, you have kids you make time for them. Whatever it costs. You make the time. Because you know what they say, you'll never make it up later.

ANDY I'm home quite a bit, you know... In the school holidays. I'm with them quite a lot...

JOE They need a mother, as well. Take my tip, you tell her to take some time off work. Alright?

ANDY She's an air traffic controller, Joe. She can't take time off just like that.

JOE When we were expecting Julia. Long before we knew she'd – turn out like she did, I said to Dolly, right that's it. Home for you. Next fifteen years. Home. No argument either.

ANDY No, I can imagine.

JOE Never did argue, Dolly and me. Never in thirty-two years. Not many can say that. Mind you, I tried on one or two occasions. You know, to start a row with her. Just for devilment. But she never would, Dolly. Amazing temperament, like that. Just sat quietly, let it flow over her. Or, you know, if things got really bad, just walked quietly out of the room. *(Reflecting)* I can't have been the easiest person to live with sometimes, I suppose.

ANDY She put up with you, anyway.

JOE Yes, well, I think I saw her right. You know it occurred to me earlier, watching those youngsters of yours tearing round the house...

ANDY I'm sorry, were they –?

JOE No, no, no. What I'm saying is – if things had been different – if Julia hadn't – you know, gone when she did. You two might have carried on. You and her. Those kids could have been hers. Who knows?

ANDY Yes. I suppose that's possible.

JOE Now Dolly's gone, it sort of brings it home to you. I mean, she and I, we'll have left nothing behind us at all, will we? Not a solitary thing.

ANDY Julia did, though. She left us her music. And she was part of you both. Think of it that way.

JOE You know, sometimes, just between these walls, I think that's the only thing that keeps me sane, Andy, you know.

ANDY Shouldn't we be getting back? I expect this bloke downstairs wants to shut up and go home, doesn't he?

JOE No, I sent him off. I said I'd lock up. Listen. Before you go. There's something else, I wanted to... I wanted you to hear.

ANDY What is it?

JOE It's just a tape, it's...something I've not played to anyone. I – anyway, listen for yourself...

ANDY Couldn't we hear it in the car, Joe, only –

JOE It won't take a second, I need your opinion, Andy. I'd value your opinion. Wait there.

ANDY It's just that I promised Kay and the kids that I'd be back in time for...

ANDY *tails away vainly.*

JOE *has gone off through the archway.*

JOE *(offstage)* Don't fret, they'll be alright. Mrs Henderson's making them tea, don't worry.

ANDY *(calling)* If it's anything like that lunch...

JOE *(offstage)* No, she doesn't believe in half portions, Mrs Henderson – She's from the right end of the country. Like me. Just a second.

ANDY *stands aimlessly for a second, sighs to himself and then steps over the rope and into the room itself for the first time.*

ANDY *(to himself)* God. It's freezing in here. It never used to be as cold as this.

He stops at the desk and looks at the manuscript on the desk. He laughs.

JOE *returns.*

JOE Right. Ready to go.

ANDY I didn't know she wrote *Greensleeves*.

JOE Eh?

ANDY *(indicating the manuscript)* This. It's the music for *Greensleeves*. I didn't know Julia wrote that.

JOE Oh, well. We're not putting the genuine item out. Not any more. Little buggers nick everything. Music, pens, pencils, india rubbers. Soon as your back's turned they're under that rope. I tell you, they'd have made off with that bloody bed if we hadn't screwed it down. I mean, I don't know what's happening these days, do you? Whole place has gone stark bonkers. You know in that village of ours, someone made off with a belisha beacon the other day. Ten foot tall with a damn orange ball. Chopped it down like a tree in the middle of the night.

ANDY Yes, it's a problem. I don't know how one tackles it.

JOE One shoots them, that's what one does.

ANDY Yes, well... That's a solution.

JOE That's my solution.

ANDY The trouble is we always end up shooting the wrong people, Joe. We're almost certain to miss the beacon stealer and hit the old lady who's looking for somewhere to cross the road.

JOE *(unable to follow this)* Well. Be that as it may. Listen to this. Are you ready? Now you recall the original commentary? The one you were listening to just now?

ANDY Yes.

JOE Well, that was a copy. A third copy from the original master. I replaced that two days ago. Now, before that have been two earlier versions. Both supposedly identical – both again taken from the master – but listen to this... Now, no one's heard this except you and me – Well, except Jack who let us in and he won't say anything to anyone, he's a miserable old sod. Anyway. Listen to this. You have to listen carefully, though, on this first one...

He presses the red button. The commentary starts up again.

WOMAN Finally, this is the place where I spent most of my time while I was at college here. The house was then a student residence and this was my room when I was at the university, as a result of winning my music scholarship.

ANDY *(after a second, over the commentary)* What are we listening for?

JOE Just a minute, just a minute.

They listen.

She is like her, isn't she? Very like Julia. Could be Julia. Not quite but close...

ANDY The only thing wrong is – I can't remember Julia ever talking as slowly as this.

JOE *(smiling)* No, you're right. Sixteen to the dozen, wasn't she? Dolly used to say that sometimes, if you'd had a conversation with Julia you needed a lie down for half an hour...

WOMAN *(continuing)* It was a considerable change after my home in Otley, West Yorkshire, I can tell you. Quite modest, isn't it? I wonder what Mozart would have made of it! Amazing to think that it was at that small table which you can see there that I wrote over thirty of my hundred plus compositions including my three string quartets, an unfinished symphony for orchestra and solo wind instruments, and two of the three movements from my very popular Ridings Suite. All

in pencil with not a piano in sight, mark you. Just me and
Emily – that's my favourite teddy bear sitting on the bed
there...

JOE *(at this point, over the continuing narration)* That's the
third bloody teddy bear we've been through and all... The
next person who tries it is in for a shock, I can tell you.

ANDY What have you done? Filled it with explosives?

JOE The next best thing. Hang on. It's coming up in a minute.
Listen. You have to listen carefully...

They listen intently.

WOMAN *(continuing, meanwhile)* I always preferred to work
straight on to the manuscript, often working till three or
four o'clock in the morning while the ideas were still fresh
and buzzing around in my brain – and besides if you'd ever
heard my piano playing you'd know why.

*Under the next, on the recording, faintly but quite
distinctly, is the sound of a* WOMAN's *laughter. It is
not a happy laugh.*

I lived here for nearly eighteen months, seeing the occasional
visitor or rushing off for lectures or a tutorial but, in between,
mostly just doing what I loved best of all, sitting here with
my head full of music, writing away for dear life – I suppose
that's what I lived for, really. My music.

The tape stops.

JOE Could you hear it?

ANDY Laughter.

JOE Right.

ANDY Someone laughing.

JOE Not anyone laughing. Her laughing... Julia laughing...

ANDY Oh, come on...

JOE Julia laughing. It was Julia.

ANDY Be sensible...

JOE Who else was it, for God's sake?

ANDY Well... I don't know. Anyone. What about the woman who made the recording?

JOE What? You mean she came back later and had a laugh at it...?

ANDY No, but – maybe she had more than one go at it. Maybe she did an earlier take and she went wrong and she laughed and they did it again – only the original is still there.

JOE I checked. They said it was a professional digital recording. There's no way that could have happened. It was checked.

ANDY Well, they'd say that...

JOE Then why isn't it on the original? Tell me that. Why just on this particular copy?

ANDY Well, maybe it...maybe it happened afterwards. It's possible. We had trouble at school with our sound system. When we did Ruddigore. We kept picking up Classic FM.

JOE Listen to it, man. Does that in a month of Sundays sound like bloody Classic FM?

ANDY No, I'm not saying... All I'm saying is – there's an explanation... There must be.

JOE Alright. Wait there. Listen to this next one. Now, this only happened ten days ago. Wait there.

*JOE has gone out. **ANDY** shrugs and shakes his head. He wanders around the room. He reaches the bedside table.*

(offstage) Sit down if you want to. Just don't try to pick anything up.

ANDY, *who was about to do so, hastily moves his hand away. Suddenly he shivers, despite his overcoat. He looks* *towards the door of the room as if to detect the source of a draught.* JOE *returns again.*

Now listen to this. This was the second replacement copy we put in. The second copy from the same master tape. I've started it later in. Listen to this.

JOE *presses the red button. The recording starts up in mid-sentence.*

WOMAN ...mostly just doing what I loved best of all, sitting here with my head full of music, writing away for dear life – I suppose that's what I lived for, really. My music.

A brief silence on the recording. Then quite distinctly, a WOMAN*'s voice similar but not the same: –.*

(in a whisper, increasingly desperate) No...no...

MAN It was in this same room that on Tuesday, February 16th 1982, at the age of 19, Julia Lukin was found dead...

WOMAN *(in a whisper)* No...

MAN The victim of an overdose of alcohol and drugs – the tragic end to a brilliant life.

WOMAN *(in a whisper)* No...

MAN We can only be thankful that her music lives on after her...

WOMAN *(in a long, drawn out whisper)* Noooooo...

A pause.

ANDY *(a bit shaken)* Bloody hell.

JOE What's that then, Radio 1?

ANDY There must be an explanation. I mean, a real explanation. Not the sort of explanation you're thinking of. A technical one.

Pause.

There has to be.

Pause.

I mean. There does.

JOE Little Miss Mozart. That's what they used to call her, you know. The popular press. Little Miss Mozart...

ANDY I don't think it was a label she cared for very much.

JOE I never knew why she didn't. He was the best, wasn't he? Mozart? Top man. The gaffer. She should have been proud...

ANDY I think she felt the comparison was more on account of her age than her music. She might just as easily have been Little Miss Mendelssohn except none of those idiots would have been able to spell it.

JOE Little Miss Mendelssohn. No, it doesn't sound as good, does it? Anyway, I told her. She should have been proud. I mean, it would have been like me being called... I don't know... I don't think there's an equivalent in contract industrial fencing suppliers, but you know what I mean.

A silence.

ANDY *(quietly)* You have to give this up, Joe.

JOE Listen. We were neither of us that special, let's face it, Dolly and me. OK, so I've done pretty well in business and I've built it up from nothing and for a working class lad with a tenth of an education that's not bad going, but all the same. Ordinary. Essentially, ordinary people. If you'd crept into our house during the night and swapped us both for someone else, chances are no one would ever have noticed the difference...

ANDY Now, come on...

JOE Well, a little bit exaggerated but not a lot. But I'll tell you. Then something came along right out of the blue that did make us different. We produced Julia. God knows how. God knows where from. I'm three parts tone deaf and Dolly only liked flamenco. But suddenly there she was,

Little Miss Mozart. And suddenly we're different for the first time in our lives. Between us we've – made – Julia. Two or three years old, there she is, banging out tunes on toy xylophones and kiddies' keyboards – screaming every time we switched the radio on or tried to play the hi-fi. She couldn't listen to music as a baby, you know, she couldn't bear it.

ANDY Yes. You can understand that.

JOE We thought at first it was just our sort of music, you know, that upset her. Pop music, you know. But no, it was everything. Beethoven – Bach – even Mozart... Good music as well...

ANDY She told me once that when she was a kid, it was like... well, the equivalent of being blinded with light or colour. Like staring into the sun. Like giving a baby rich food. It actually made her feel sick...

JOE Well, later on we saw that, yes. But Dolly and I, at first, I don't mind saying we were a bit frightened. We reckoned she was, like, retarded. She often wouldn't speak. She was backward in reading and writing. The school said we don't know what we're going to do with her. She tried to bite the other kids and, as a result, she got bullied – then she wouldn't go to school at all. We were beside ourselves with worry. And then came all this music. From this tiny little girl. Music and more music. Like she was bursting with it. Scribbling it down – like it was something she badly needed to tell someone – in her own way, you know, to start with until she taught herself to write it properly – and we thought, well, this is all fine and good – but it's not going to get her very far in life, is it? – just sitting at home writing music all day – I mean, it was not even as if it were pop music – I mean, you can make a bit of money at that if you're lucky – but this was all, you know, cello sonatas and wind ensembles... And then this woman came to see us from the education people and she was a bit different, you could tell she was a cut above the others, and she says, you've certainly got a problem here, Mr Lukin, and I said, you're telling us that? Tell us what we do about it. And she says, I'm sorry there's nothing you can do about a genius, I'm afraid, you just have to try and live with them. And suddenly it all made sense, you see. And she said to us, my advice to you, Mr and Mrs Lukin, is to try and enjoy Julia while you can. Because they come this way but once.

Pause.

And that's what we always tried to do. Enjoy her. There we were, living with a celebrity. They all came running. Newspapers, radio, film crews, TV commercials, Sunday supplements... Little Miss Mozart. *(Smiling)* Don't know who made that one up. It sort of stuck. There was one time we did this TV chat show. Live, you know. Early evening. Julia was, well, about six years old at the time. And they announced her and we brought her on, Dolly and me. I mean, we were just there for show, they didn't want to talk to us really. And the idea was, Julia was going to talk to the bloke first and then she was going away for the rest of the programme and sit in a dressing room on her own and write a piece of piano music there and then. Just a short bit. And at the end, they had this concert pianist on – famous bloke, forgotten his name – Giorgio, George? Something like that – and anyway, he was going to take what she'd written and play it for them, sight read it – as a sort of, you know, grand finale to the programme. Only I think this pianist, he was expecting something a bit simple seeing as she was only six years old. And he's not a very pleasant man, not at all, you know, superior, and I could tell Julia hadn't taken to him. And when she comes out again at the end, she's written, you know, about ten sides of manuscript – and I can see this bloke going, you know, bloody hellfire. And he starts to try to play it and there's sweat running down his dinner jacket and he's battling away there with all these – what do you call them? – sharps and flats and key changes – and he's – wooh – he's in a proper tangle. He said after the programme was over, he said, bloody hell, he said, give me Stockhouse any day of the week.

They laugh.

Was it Stockhouse?

ANDY Stockhausen, I think.

JOE Stockhausen. That's the one.

ANDY But you enjoyed her. That's the point.

JOE Yes, I think we did.

ANDY Then don't you think it's time you let her go?

JOE No. Because if you want the truth, I don't think it's over. There are still questions about her – particularly about her death – the reason she died that haven't been answered.

ANDY The reason she died –

JOE Yes, I know – accidental overdose – we know all that. Girl genius who can't even follow the instructions on a bottle of pills... And it's a load of eyewash. Always has been, you know it. Cover up from start to finish...

ANDY The only thing they were covering up was suicide, Joe. The way they usually try to do. That's the probable alternative...

JOE That's even more ridiculous. The girl had everything to live for. She had her future like a – six lane motorway – stretching out in front of her. The reason you kill yourself is when you're facing a damn great brick wall. That's when you decide to kill yourself. When there's nowhere for you to go.

ANDY Who builds the wall, though? That's the point.

JOE Meaning she did?

ANDY Possibly.

JOE Bollocks.

ANDY *shrugs.*

Why are you saying all this, anyway? You knew her. You knew her as well as I did. You were with her right up to the end, practically. Did she ever mention suicide to you?

ANDY No. I mean, you tend to read things in after the event – but nothing – no – not really. Not at the time.

JOE She may have been a genius – a race apart – but she was still my daughter. And I'm telling you, suicide is not part of our family's language. We're fighters.

ANDY Well, if you won't accept suicide and you don't think it was accidental, that doesn't leave a lot else, does it? Unless you think that someone crept in here and forced pills down her throat.

JOE I think something of the sort might have happened.

ANDY What are you talking about?

JOE Come on, she was amongst students. They're always messing around with drugs, students. They're permanently at it. It's – what do they say – part of their culture... ? You pick up a student and shake him, he's got so many pills in him he rattles...

ANDY There are drugs and drugs, Joe.

JOE They're all drugs.

ANDY You usually take them to get high. Or to stay awake for exams. You don't get high on twenty five sleeping pills, you go to sleep – permanently – even Julia knew that...

JOE How could she? They weren't even her pills – they established that. Somebody brought them here. The prescription label had been torn off – they never found out whose they were, that's the whole point. She'd been out somewhere, she'd been drinking – we know that – she came home, almost certainly with someone – some friends she'd met – who most probably brought the pills with them – persuaded her it might be a bit of fun to take them – see what happened – she's not used to them – it all goes wrong – they panic and run away... That's what I think happened. Something like that.

ANDY But who? They never found anyone.

JOE Well, you're clear. You were legless at a party, weren't you? With about ten witnesses. Most of them lying on top of you by the sound of it. There was someone else though, wasn't there? Another man – apart from you?

ANDY There possibly was...

JOE Possibly? What do you mean, 'possibly'? You told the police at the time there was. That Julia had told you...

ANDY She mentioned him – occasionally...

JOE But never his name?

ANDY No. She made a special point of that.

JOE He was married, that's my theory...

ANDY I don't really know if he even existed. Not now, Joe. I was jealous enough at the time to believe it, but – I think now she probably invented him – just to – you know – wind me up. She used to call him her secret admirer. I'd come round sometimes and she wouldn't be in. Even though she said she would be. Where were you last night, I'd say to her? Oh, just with my secret admirer. She used to tease me quite a lot like that. I was incredibly – I don't know – inexperienced. Gullible. Pathetic, really... But then women can always... Can't they? When they feel like it. You know, turn you inside out?

JOE Not me they don't.

ANDY Well, you're very lucky...

JOE Does Kay do that? To you?

ANDY Well, you know. No. Well, now and then. I mean... You know. Not like Julia, anyway. I've never met anyone else like Julia, that's for sure. Maybe it's being your first... I told you I was innocent. We sat next to each other in this lecture. That's how we met. This strange girl suddenly there next to me, fidgeting and muttering. Scratching. Baking hot day, she's bundled up like an eskimo. Not beautiful – not even that pretty really – but burning. Restless. Wasting her time here. And meanwhile, there's this poor bloke up there on the podium, some visiting lecturer or other, quite distinguished probably, doing his best to enlighten us further about the finer points of orchestral composition – and she's shaking her head and banging the desk – and in the end she's making such a racket the lecturer calls up to her and says, young lady, I'm sure that for you this is probably a very elementary voyage but do please try and paddle along with the rest of us. And she says to him, sir, I'd be happy to, only at present we appear to be captained by *Das Fliegende Holländer*... *(He laughs)*

JOE *laughs briefly, then looks puzzled.*

JOE No, I don't get that.

ANDY Sorry. *The Flying Dutchman.*

JOE Oh yes. She could speak her mind.

ANDY Anyway. She got thrown out of the lecture and I followed her. Love at first sight. For me at any rate. *(He smiles to himself)*

JOE I'd better put the proper tape back.

ANDY Then can we go home for tea?

JOE In a minute.

JOE *goes offstage.* ANDY *flaps his arms to warm himself.*

ANDY I'm getting really frozen here.

JOE *(offstage)* Something else to do first.

ANDY Not another tape.

JOE *(offstage)* You don't reckon them, then? These tapes?

ANDY As what?

JOE *(offstage)* As being – what they appear to be? Julia. Trying to contact us. Contact me.

ANDY No, I don't. I think that's dangerous rubbish. I don't believe it for a minute.

JOE *returns.*

JOE Dangerous?

ANDY Yes.

JOE To tamper, you mean? With the unknown?

ANDY Yes. Not because I think spooks are going to jump out at you. That Julia's suddenly going to step out of the woodwork – but I think it can do dangerous things to your own mind. Set up false hopes, expectations. She's dead, Joe. Julia's dead. I was the one who found her in here, remember? And I can tell you she was very, very dead... Alright? Now, I know that may sound cruel but accept it. You have to accept that.

JOE I do.

ANDY Well.

JOE That doesn't mean she's not trying to contact me, does it? Trying to tell me something important?

ANDY Oh, God. Why should she bother?

JOE What do you mean?

ANDY Accepting the hypothesis – If she's dead but she still exists as an individual...which I don't personally happen to believe either, but that's by the by...then she must be somewhere else presumably. Now, she's either gone to a better place, in which case she's far too busy being happy to bother with us – or she's gone to a worse place – where I doubt they let them out to visit...

JOE You want to make jokes about it, make jokes, I don't care.

ANDY I'm sorry. It's just I have trouble believing in most of what's happening in this world, Joe.

JOE Let me show you something. You say you're cold.

ANDY Bloody freezing. And I would dearly love to go home now and see my kids.

JOE Just come over here. This side of the rope.

ANDY Why?

JOE Just come here. Stand next to me for a second.

ANDY does so.

Well?

ANDY Yes.

JOE Warmer?

ANDY Yes.

JOE Considerably warmer?

ANDY Considerably. But then all that proves is that –

JOE Now, put your hand out over the other side of the rope. Go on, like that.

JOE demonstrates. ANDY follows suit.

Cold. Right?

He grabs ANDY's arm and moves it several times rapidly from one side of the rope to the other.

Warm – cold – warm – cold – warm – cold – alright? Yes, I know what you're going to say. This proves we've discovered that ornamental rope has extraordinary properties of insulation. Hooray, we're rich.

ANDY *(muttering)* There's a logical explanation.

JOE You should get that put on your tombstone. No, it's always been like that. Ever since we knocked through. Knocked this wall down. We tried everything. Fan heaters. Oil stoves. It's like it just – the room just sucks away all the heat.

ANDY I had digs like that once.

JOE Garn. Get on with you. Smart ass bloody public school boys.

ANDY Minor public school, do you mind?

A bell rings loudly.

ANDY *jumps.*

(startled) What the hell was that?

JOE No idea. There'll be a logical explanation, though, don't worry.

ANDY No, what was it?

JOE Front doorbell.

ANDY Who?

JOE The bloke we've come here to meet, that's who.

JOE *starts to leave.*

ANDY What bloke? I want to go home, Joe.

JOE You'll get home, they'll save you a butterfly cake, don't worry. Wait there.

JOE *leaves.*

ANDY *paces about agitatedly.*

ANDY *(looking at his watch)* I've missed my programme now.

From outside the door of the room the sound of footsteps running down a flight of wooden stairs. They could be a woman's.

ANDY *looks up, a little startled.*

He moves towards the door to investigate. As he does so, **KEN** *appears in the doorway. In his late forties, he is a pleasant, cheerful, unassuming man.*

KEN Hallo there.

ANDY *jumps.*

Is this where we're met?

ANDY *(recovering)* Hallo.

KEN Hallo. Ken Chase. How do you do?

ANDY Hallo.

KEN You're –?

ANDY Andy. Andy Rollinson...

KEN Pleased to meet you, Mr Rollinson. How do you do?

A pause.

Quite a pleasant day. Thought it would rain earlier. But no. It was not to be. We were spared that, at least.

ANDY Yes.

KEN Had quite enough of that for one month...

ANDY Yes, indeed...

KEN ...thank you very much. No, it's brisk but it's pleasant out there. If you keep walking. Can't afford to stand around, mind you.

ANDY Did you walk, then?

KEN No, I came in the car.

Pause.

Mr Lukin's just on his way. He's making a phone call. He told me to find my own way up. Quite an impressive building. Like a rabbit warren, isn't it?

ANDY Have we met? I feel I've met you before.

KEN I can't recall offhand. But we may have done.

ANDY It was just...probably not.

KEN It's possible. I meet quite a number of people in my line of work.

ANDY Do you? What line is that?

KEN I'm a mortuary attendant.

ANDY Ah.

KEN Up at the city mortuary.

ANDY Is that interesting?

KEN Yes – it is, funnily enough. Wasn't my original line, of course. I had an enforced career change midway and this post came up and I decided to give it a go. Bit of a dead end job, I thought, to start with. *(He laughs)*

ANDY *smiles weakly.*

But then you get involved, you know, as you do. And suddenly it's all very interesting.

ANDY Yes.

JOE *returns.*

KEN Ah.

JOE Oh, you found it. Good. Have you introduced yourselves?

ANDY Yes, indeed. Mr Chase was just telling me about his job.

JOE Really? What do you do then?

KEN I'm a mortuary attendant.

JOE Are you? I didn't know that.

KEN Well, I didn't mention it in my letter. I didn't really think it was germane.

JOE No, well. Probably not. Well, this is Mr Rollinson. Andy. Who's an old friend of mine and who – No, hang on. See how good you are. *(Indicating* ANDY*)* Looking at him, what do you think he does for a living.

KEN Ah. Oh, a challenge, yes.

JOE Have a guess.

KEN Well, I've only just met you...but... *(He concentrates)* I sense...do I sense music? Yes, music...

JOE That's good.

KEN Am I right so far?

ANDY *(guardedly)* Yes.

KEN But – not a musician as such, I think...?

ANDY Well, that's open to question...

KEN No. Beg your pardon. Rephrase that. I meant you're not a professional musician per se. You're not in a band or an orchestra. I think you're possibly a teacher. A music teacher? Am I right?

JOE Brilliant.

ANDY Very good. How did you guess that?

KEN Ah, well. Elementary really. There are traces of chalk under your fingernails and what with the trombone sticking out of your pocket... *(He laughs)* No, to be serious...

JOE Mr Chase is a – psychic – is that the word?

KEN Yes, that'll do. That'll do. I don't object to that.

JOE Would you describe yourself as a medium?

KEN No, no. Certainly not. No, that's quite different. That's an altogether different field. No, my area is more – let's say being able to tune to certain vibrations, moods, feelings. It's nothing very special. In fact, I suspect most of us have that latent ability. Only some of us choose to deny it.

ANDY Yes.

KEN Maybe through fear...

ANDY Maybe through common sense.

KEN *(unoffended)* Maybe. Who knows? It's certainly not a very precise science, I have to be the first to admit. I mean, there are some people or locations where I just draw a complete blank. Nothing at all. Total silence.

JOE How do you hear it, then? Like words in your head?

KEN No – when I say silence – it's more images – like tiny fragments of pictures – they don't always make sense very often. I mean, quite trivial, sometimes. Like I said to the wife the other day, we were on the way to the supermarket for the weekly shop and I said, Kath, why do I keep sensing running water – a lot of gushing? And she said, oh my goodness, I left the tap running in the sink... Near disaster.

ANDY Useful.

KEN Can be, yes. Can be. And then again...

JOE What?

KEN There are things that you catch a sense of – that you know are happening...have happened...are even about to happen... and there's nothing you can do about it. Not a thing. That can be frustrating. I sometimes think that then, on those occasions, it's better not to know at all. But you don't have the choice, you see. It's like being in a room with a hundred conversations and you'll hear whatever it is you happen to hear. Only if it was as simple as that, at least then you could cover your ears. There's nothing you can do when it's in your head. Or nothing we've discovered so far, anyway.

JOE So. What do you sense now? At this moment?

KEN Now? Well, nothing very much at the moment. It's very peaceful, *(Indicating the rope barrier)* May I...?

JOE Of course...

ANDY Just a minute. Excuse me. Joe, what's going on?

JOE I've invited Mr Chase here as a result of a letter he wrote me –

KEN Oh, I do apologise, Mr Rollinson, I didn't realise you didn't know why I was here. I assumed you did. I am sorry.

ANDY I don't know anything about anything. I no longer even know why I'm here. I thought it was to have a look round the Centre. It now appears there are other motives entirely...

JOE Alright, alright, Andy, don't get yourself in a state...

ANDY I just want to know what's going on here.

JOE I'll explain it to you. I'll explain.

ANDY Well, you better bloody had.

JOE *(to* KEN*)* Excuse us.

KEN That's quite alright. Perhaps I shouldn't have said it was peaceful. I appear to have started something. *(He laughs)*

JOE I need you here, Andy, because you're a part of this. Even if you don't believe in what I'm doing, even if you think I'm completely barmy and I know you do, you still have to be here. So bear with me. Please.

ANDY And what is it you are doing, Joe? Precisely?

JOE I want to know why she died. That's all. I've heard a lot of theories, all sorts of psychological reasons, I've had policemen and doctors and psychiatrists all trotting out their favourite scenarios or whatever they call them and they all amount to a load of so much boiled cabbage. Now, I don't know if Mr. Chase here can do what he says he can – I'll take his word for it because he seems a genuine enough bloke – but if he can throw even a glimmer of light on why my nineteen year old daughter, who was dearer to me than anything in this world, died in this room twelve years ago, I'll be eternally grateful to him.

ANDY *(wearily)* What's the point now?

JOE *(loudly)* I want to know. Alright? I was her father. I have a right to know.

Silence.

KEN *(tentatively indicating the rope again)* May I...

JOE Of course. Sorry, Mr Chase...

KEN Ken, please. Ken.

JOE Alright. Joe.

KEN Joe, right.

JOE Andy.

KEN Andy. Yes.

> KEN *climbs over the rope. As soon as he does so, he recoils as if hit by a shock wave.*

> Oh! *(He sways)* Oh, dear.

JOE *(anxiously)* Alright?

KEN Yes, yes. Oh, dear. Yes. It hits you, doesn't it? Quite a shock. Just stepping over the rope.

JOE The cold, you mean?

KEN Is it cold? Oh, yes it is, isn't it? Very. That as well.

ANDY As well as what?

KEN As well as – the unhappiness. Oh, dear. Such terrible unhappiness. Oh, dear. *(He stands for a moment)* You must excuse me. I didn't quite anticipate this, I'm sorry.

JOE Do you need to sit down?

KEN No, I'll be fine. I'll be fine in a minute. It's just getting used to it. Would you mind if I look around?

JOE Please.

> JOE *and* ANDY *stand back to allow* KEN *to make a tour of inspection.*

KEN *(regarding the room)* Yes. Yes. Yes. *(Pause)* Yes.

JOE Do you need anything?

KEN No, no... *(Indicating the door of the room)* May I?

JOE It doesn't go anywhere.

KEN Oh, nor it does. Brick wall. What a surprise. Yes, I see, so you opened up at that end...

JOE Knocked through from next door...

KEN The original wall being where that rope is now?

JOE Exactly.

KEN Yes, that makes sense. That explains the incredible change. I mean, that side of the rope it's very peaceful. Must have been a monastery or something, I should imagine... *(He laughs)*

JOE I think it was an ironmonger's.

KEN Ah well. Obviously happy in their work, weren't they? ...So you bricked this up, I see...?

JOE Yes. There's no need to go through there now.

ANDY You kept the stairs though?

JOE Where?

ANDY Through here. The original stairs? They're still there?

JOE No, I'm saying, there was no need for them. That area's now an air conditioning plant. We had to put in new fire escapes, anyway, so we removed those stairs altogether.

ANDY I see.

JOE Why do you ask?

ANDY No reason. Just curious.

KEN *(having finished his examination)* Well.

JOE Well?

KEN As I say, there's a very great feeling coming from the room... very strong. But I would say – she's not here. She's not in the room with us. Not at present.

ANDY Glad to hear it.

KEN But she is close. She's not far away. I'd say she's in the building certainly.

JOE Julia?

KEN Yes. I assume it's her. Yes. A young woman, anyway.

ANDY *(impatiently)* Oh, come on...

JOE Look, just give the bloke a chance, Andy. Just give him a chance...

ANDY It's a load of rubbish. You know it... I'm sorry...

JOE I'm prepared to listen to him that's all... What's wrong with that?

ANDY If you weren't so emotionally involved you'd see it for yourself. You'd see he was having you on... He's a phoney.

JOE How the hell do you expect him to do anything when you won't even give him a chance? – I'm sorry Mr – Ken. I'm sorry. Excuse us.

KEN That's quite alright, Joe, it's not a problem. It happens occasionally. People get frightened and then they get a bit angry, you know...

ANDY *(angrily)* I'm not frightened...

KEN *(to JOE)* It's the unknown. It's only natural.

ANDY And if I am angry it's because you are exploiting this man who is emotionally vulnerable and – highly susceptible to this sort of rubbish. And it is not only wrong, it is downright immoral and irresponsible to take advantage of people like this. That's all. Alright?

Pause.

KEN I'm sorry you feel that way.

JOE I don't know why you're quite so angry, I don't at all, Andy.

ANDY Because I care about you. And people taking advantage of you.

JOE Is that the reason?

ANDY Yes.

JOE Well, I believe you. I'm sorry, Ken. Have we – you know, broken your mood or something...?

KEN No, no, no, no, no. It doesn't work like that. That's perfectly alright. I mean, as I say, one does get antagonism – but it doesn't really affect things. It's not like a seance. It just tends to slow things down rather.

ANDY How much money are you paying him for this?

KEN Paying me? Nothing at all. I wouldn't dream of it.

JOE Ken wrote to me a week or so ago. He said he'd been round the centre as an ordinary visitor with his family – when was it? A couple of Saturdays ago, wasn't it?

KEN That's right. Whole party of us. Kath my wife, my son Alec, our daughter-in-law Tracy and our grandson Darren who's eight years old next Tuesday. And I got a sort of feeling then – off the building, you know – not as strong as now, because I wasn't able to go into this area, of course, but strong enough and I thought no more about it. And then I came across an interview that Joe here gave in the local paper. Giving his reasons why he opened this place and so on. And I thought maybe I should write and tell him, you see. I mean, he was perfectly at liberty not to reply. You really mustn't think I'm here to make money, Andy. That couldn't be farther from the truth.

ANDY I'm sorry.

KEN You were very close to her, too, weren't you? To Julie?

ANDY Yes. Yes, I was.

KEN I thought so. Well, we must try and get to the truth of things, mustn't we? In so far as we are able. In so far as she'll allow us to.

JOE What are you going to do? Try and get through to her?

KEN No, no. I keep saying, this is not a seance. That's not in my gift, I'm afraid. I'm not able to hold conversations with the departed. I can't possibly manage things like that. That's very specialised and given to very few. Far fewer, I suspect, than some would have us believe. As I say, mine's a very ordinary gift. I'm sure either of you could do it if you put your mind to it. It's just a matter of just – well, opening yourself up, really. We're like radio sets. But mostly we're all switched on to transmit, you see. Even when we think we're listening to each other, we're not really. We're actually busy thinking up what we're going to say, even before the other person's finished saying what they're saying. You catch yourself doing it next time. You'll see what I mean. Now with what I do, the only thing about that is, you not only have to stop yourself transmitting, like that radio, you actually have to switch yourself over to receive mode. Because also like a radio, you can't receive while you're transmitting, you see.

JOE How do you switch over?

KEN Well, practice really. It gets easier the more you do it. I suspect some of us find it comes more naturally than others. It helps if you're a reasonably passive sort of person. I shouldn't imagine that people with great vitality find it all that easy. And you need to start early in life, too, I reckon. The older you get the more that switch rusts over. I mean, that's just my personal theory. My grandson Darren, he can do it. He can tell you where his second hand lego came from, who owned it last. But my son Alec, no way. He's here, there and everywhere. Permanently broadcasting he is. Got more transmitters than Bush House. But lots of children have it. Until we come along and tell them to stop being so stupid. So they do. Only I sometimes think we're the stupid ones, really. I'm sorry, I do beg your pardon. Get me going on this I'm away for hours.

ANDY No, it's very interesting. So you reckon children are natural, so called receivers?

KEN I believe they are, yes.

ANDY And say, take my kids – they could wander around picking up all sorts of signals.

KEN Oh, yes.

ANDY But not all of them good, presumably.

KEN Indeed no. On the contrary. For every good thought there's at least one evil one. Well, harmful let's say, anyway.

ANDY So how do we control that?

KEN Well, you start by trying to share them with them. Like you would a book. If you want to know what your children are reading you'd better read it too, hadn't you?

ANDY That's an interesting theory.

JOE There you are. You've got him believing now.

ANDY No, I still think it's load of rubbish but it's quite interesting.

JOE Well, we'd better get going, hadn't we? I phoned them by the way, Andy – that's what I was doing just now – letting them know we'd be a bit late. I spoke to Kay.

ANDY Was she alright?

JOE Yes, she sounded – alright. Can be a bit terse like on the phone, can't she?

ANDY Sometimes.

JOE Probably her air traffic control manner. She gives you the feeling you're some cack-handed pilot coming in at the wrong altitude...

ANDY Well...

JOE You can always stay over, you know. All of you. I mean, it's no trouble, we've plenty of rooms... I'm sure Mrs Henderson would –

ANDY No, honestly... Please. No.

JOE Well, just a thought. Ken, yes. Sorry. Now, talk us through it. What do you want us to do?

KEN You? Oh, nothing very much you need do. Just give me a moment's quiet if you could.

ANDY *(dryly)* While you throw the switch.

KEN *(unaware)* That's right. Oh, just one thing. I mean, nothing's probably going to happen, don't get me wrong but – this is just my little blurb, I always do this – nothing's probably going to happen but, well, we are dealing with things which are – unusual, shall we say. Out of the ordinary. Now, in all my years nothing's ever happened that's been at all dangerous or even particularly frightening. Providing you're prepared. But – things do happen occasionally – that can't immediately be explained and – well, just keep your minds open if you can, that's all I'm saying. The only thing that can hurt yourself in the end is your own self.

JOE Right. *(To* ANDY*)* Are you listening to that?

ANDY Yes. I've got the message, thank you.

KEN Right.

He concentrates for a second.

Oh. The feeling's still – very strong in here. Poor girl. Poor, poor girl.

A silence. KEN *stands silently, his eyes closed.* JOE *and* ANDY *watch him.*

(quietly) It's getting colder, isn't it? Can you feel it?

JOE *(softly)* Yes. Is she here?

KEN No, no, she's not. But she's close... She's probably not even aware of us. We'd be like ghosts to her...

Pause.

JOE *has closed his eyes.*

It helps sometimes if I can hold something that belonged to her. Something personal. *(Seeing the teddy bear on the bed)* May I?

JOE *(his eyes still closed)* Help yourself.

> **KEN** *attempts to pick up the bear. It is attached to a security wire, invisible till now, threaded through the counterpane.*

> *A terrific din as the alarm goes off all round them. All three are very startled.*

ANDY *(an involuntary yell)* Wah!

KEN *(yelling above the din)* What's happening?

JOE *(shouting)* It's the alarm. Sorry, I meant to switch it off before we started. Hang on. I'll go and do it. Leave the bear alone. Wait till I switch off.

> **JOE** *hurries off through the arch.*

> **ANDY** *and* **KEN** *stand waiting for the din to stop, which eventually it does.*

ANDY *(once silence is restored)* That should have frightened her off, anyway.

KEN You don't have an awful lot of faith in me, do you?

ANDY I think you believe it. That bit's genuine. I just don't believe what you believe, that's all.

KEN Ah well. That's at the root of most of our problems, isn't it?

ANDY I know you from somewhere. I know I do.

KEN Possibly.

> **JOE** *returns.*

JOE Sorry. My fault. Has that ruined the mood?

KEN No. Hasn't done my eardrums any good but I think we can carry on. *(Indicating the bear)* May I?

JOE Yes. Wait a tick. There's a hook here, I'll just...

> **JOE** *unfastens the bear from the security wire.*

I've switched everything off now. Nothing else should disturb us.

JOE *hand the bear to* KEN.

KEN Thank you. *(Holding the bear)* Oh, yes. Oh dear, yes...

JOE What?

KEN I'm beginning to get all sorts of pictures, all sorts of things... She's unhappy...she's terribly unhappy...

JOE But why? Why?

KEN It's difficult to explain, it's...

JOE Why is she unhappy? We loved her. Doesn't she know we loved her?

KEN She knows. She knows that... She loves you.

JOE Then what did we do?

KEN It's not you, it's...

JOE Well, who is it? Is it Andy? Who?

KEN No, it's not Andy...she loves Andy...she can't show it but she loves him, too...

JOE Well, who else? Is it this other man?

KEN No, no...

JOE There's another man somewhere, isn't there?

KEN No...

JOE Her secret admirer?

KEN *(becoming increasingly agitated)* No, no, you've got it wrong. It's not the men. It's not the men. It's not the men.

JOE Then what the hell is it? What makes a girl of nineteen kill herself like that – without coming to us for help...

KEN You wouldn't understand...

JOE ...without even trying to tell me...

KEN ...you wouldn't understand...you wouldn't understand...

JOE Go on, try me. Tell me what the bloody hell made her do that to us?

KEN It's the music. It's just the music...that's all...

JOE The music? Julia! What do you mean the music...?

KEN It's – like a great cloud in front of the sun... *(With a cry of pain)* It's blotting out her life...

A silence. KEN *stands swaying slightly. Emotionally very affected by this, as is* JOE.

ANDY *watches silently and impassively...*

JOE *(softly)* What does that mean? I don't know what that means.

KEN Sorry. That came out a little more – excitable – than usual.

ANDY You got all that from a teddy bear?

KEN Well, not literally. I mean, it could be any object. So long as it's something personal. It has to be something close to the subject. Something she related to.

ANDY Like that bear?

KEN Yes. Exactly. She obviously had some close affinity... Obviously.

JOE *(realising, quietly)* Oh, my God!

KEN Sorry?

JOE You liar. You bloody sham. I should break your neck, you cheap, conniving bastard...

JOE *moves towards* KEN *threateningly.*

KEN *(alarmed)* Now, hold on, hold on. Just a minute. What are you doing?

JOE This wasn't even hers. This wasn't even hers, you bastard.

He snatches the bear back from **KEN**.

I ought to stuff it down your throat...

KEN *backs away and falls on to the bed.* **JOE** *stands over him.* **ANDY** *intervenes.*

ANDY Easy... Joe...easy...

KEN *(meanwhile)* I don't know what you mean. I don't know what you're talking about...

JOE I'm saying this wasn't hers. Hers was nicked three weeks ago.

ANDY Joe!

JOE *gives up and moves away.*

JOE Oh, come on. Why waste our time? Let's go home. And you – out. You ever come back here, I'll kill you. I promise I will.

KEN *(hoarsely)* I don't quite see what the problem is...

ANDY The problem is, old mate, that you've blown it. The great psychic teddy bear never did belong to Julia. It's a replacement. Actually a second replacement – or is it the third, I forget?

JOE Third.

ANDY So you see, it sort of all falls to the ground, doesn't it?

KEN Oh. I see. Oh, dear.

JOE What did you hope to get out of this, eh? What? Money from a grateful father? What?

KEN Peace of mind.

JOE What?

KEN My own peace of mind. And I hope yours.

JOE What are you saying?

ANDY Don't listen to him, Joe. Not any more. Please. Let's go home.

JOE Peace of mind? You were hoping to give me peace of mind? How did you hope to do that exactly? By lying to me? Did you think that was going to make things better?

KEN I have been lying to you. I admit it. I have. I'm sorry. But it wasn't all lies, you see.

JOE Oh yes. Which bits weren't then?

ANDY Joe...

KEN You see, I knew her. I knew Julie.

JOE You knew her?

KEN Yes.

JOE Am I to believe that?

KEN I used to live here in this house.

JOE Here?

KEN When it was a residence. When they all lived here. The students. I was - in the flat in the basement...

ANDY Of course. Of course. I know you now. Mr Base.

JOE Mr who?

ANDY Mr Chase in the basement. We used to call him Mr Base in the chasement, that's all... Silly.

JOE Don't tell me he was a student?

ANDY He was the caretaker.

KEN Janitor.

JOE So you knew her? You knew Julia?

KEN Oh yes. *(Indicating* ANDY*)* I remembered you, too. Soon as I came in. I thought, that's torn it. Didn't know you were going to be here, you see.

JOE Why do this to me? What were you trying to do?

KEN I was trying to put the record straight. I'm sorry. It was very wrong, I -

JOE By making things up? By raising my hopes? Pretending to be psychic and then –

KEN No, that's true, that bit's all true, I promise.

JOE Like buggery it is.

KEN It is. Believe me, please.

JOE Why? Why should I?

KEN I am psychic. To a certain extent. In that respect, I am everything I said I was. And I read your interview in the paper – the one you gave when you first opened this place – when you talked about your daughter – and I saw you on local television – and then I came here to see for myself with my family. And I did sense unhappiness. From you. From her.

JOE Well, you've done a lot to alleviate it, haven't you? Thank you very much.

KEN I knew certain things from those days about your daughter that I never said at the time.

JOE Really? What made you change your mind? You've been quiet enough for twelve years, haven't you?

KEN They were very personal things... I don't want to say any more. It all went wrong. It was a stupid idea. I've done enough damage, I'm sorry. You don't know how sorry I am. I'm really, really sorry. Please believe me.

Pause.

JOE Did you – sense her here, then? Truthfully? Did you?

KEN *(softly)* Yes.

ANDY Oh, for God's sake, we're not going through all this again...

JOE Just a minute, Andy. So it's your belief she's – her whatever – spirit is still here –?

KEN She's nearby. Yes.

JOE Not in this room?

KEN No.

JOE But near?

KEN Yes.

JOE And she's unhappy?

KEN Oh yes. She's unhappy.

JOE Why?

KEN I don't know. Because there's something not right, presumably. Maybe to do with her death. I mean, if you kill yourself, things can't be right, can they? Not for you, not for the people you leave behind? She probably realises how much she's hurt people... People who can't forgive her. I don't know.

JOE Me?

KEN Yes. And – Andy, perhaps.

JOE Andy?

KEN Yes.

ANDY You can leave me out of this...

JOE And you think she took her own life?

KEN Oh yes.

JOE Really? You seem very certain. Where the hell do you fit into all this, anyway?

KEN As I say, I knew her...

JOE You were just the caretaker...

KEN Janitor. I was a friend as well.

JOE You?

KEN *(smiling)* She used to call me her secret admirer.

ANDY Her what?

KEN It was a joke...

JOE Have I got this right? Am I to understand that while you were the caretaker of this building you had sex with my daughter? Is that what I'm hearing?

KEN No. For heaven's sake. Sex? What are you talking about? She came and sat with us, that's all. And talked and had tea and played scrabble and dominoes and ludo with me and Kath and Alec and Tracy –

JOE Who the hell are they? Students?

KEN I've told you. My wife, my son and my daughter – in – law. To be. At the time.

JOE Oh.

KEN Nothing to do with sex.

JOE No, I apologise.

KEN She was lonely, that's all.

JOE Lonely? Why?

KEN I don't know...

JOE We were less than five miles away. As soon as we heard she'd won the scholarship we moved down here. For that very reason. So she'd have us close to her.

KEN I know. She told us.

JOE *(angrily)* Then what are you talking about, lonely? Don't be so bloody daft. The fact that she very rarely came to see us, chose for some reason not to come and see us, is beside the point. Never invited us here, even. That was her choice. But she should never have been lonely. There was never a reason for her to be that. We were there. We were waiting. Always on hand. What more could we do?

KEN That's what she told us...

ANDY That she was lonely?

KEN I remember she said to us once – no one really sees me, you know... No one ever talks to me as if I were me...

ANDY And you did presumably?

KEN Well, I think we were sort of different. We never talked about her music because, well – to be honest with you – it wasn't really our sort of thing – and that seemed to suit her. When she was with us I suppose she was able to forget about it. Which may have been a nice change for her. I mean, what must it have been like with all that music in your head all the time? I asked her once. She said, Ken, usually it's lovely but there are days when you'd love to forget about it only you can't and then it's worse than a migraine.

ANDY And that bit about music blotting out her life? Was that something else she said to you?

KEN Oh, yes. She said that. I could never have made that up. But mostly we talked about ordinary things, you know. Nothing special. She was always wanting to help my wife – Kath's a dressmaker, you know – always wanted to help her with that. Kath always let her but Julie was dreadful, all fingers and thumbs. Kath never let on, though. She's a very patient person. She used to sit up half the night after Julie'd gone, you know, unpicking things. Did she ever make you a cake? Julie?

JOE No.

KEN Thank your lucky stars, you were well out of that... She'd sometimes have a go on our piano. Terrible old thing. We bought it for Alec, you know, when he went through the phase, but then he moved on to guitars and then he was into synthesisers and now he's installing satellite dishes and doesn't play a note so there you are... But Julie used to like to play, now and then. If we encouraged her. She used to laugh. She said we had the most extraordinary collection of music she'd ever come across. What did she say it was? Ecleckic? Was that it?

ANDY Eclectic.

KEN Eclectic. Beethoven, *Leaning on the Gate, Ave Maria, Sheep May Safely Graze, He Played his Ukulele as the Ship Went Down*. We had them all. A lot of it was handed on to us. We inherited them from Kath's mum, you know. Nan.

JOE She never played at home. God knows what I paid for that Steinway, she never went near it. Still there gathering dust.

KEN Maybe you didn't have the right music. *(He laughs)*

ANDY And why do you think she killed herself?

KEN I'm not sure that I know.

ANDY You said you did?

KEN No. I never said that. All I know is Julie didn't kill herself because of you. She loved you. Both of you. She really did.

JOE But she still felt lonely...?

KEN Well. She was a complicated young person, wasn't she? I mean, there could never have been anything straightforward about her, could there? Not with a brain like she had... Listen. This is what I really wanted to tell you. On the day Julie died. In the afternoon, she came down to visit at tea time. Like she often did. She'd just drop in. We were all there. She seemed very excited, she wouldn't say why. She was – well, she was never a great one for showing her emotions, was she? – Contained really, wasn't she? – At least till you got to know her properly – then she might loosen up a bit. Just a fraction. But that afternoon she was very expressive, you know – outgoing – affectionate, almost. Like a different person. And I suppose – of course, you never know whether you're reading these things in afterwards – I wondered later if she'd been saying good-bye to us. It was like she was. Maybe not. Maybe something had just happened to change her life. Whatever. We never saw her again, anyway. But on that occasion, this is the point, that was also the only time she talked about her family. About you and your wife. The only time. She said she realised how much she loved you. She said, it was odd – love was like a compliment. People like her who found it hard to give often found it equally hard to accept. But she was going to try and change all that.

Pause.

And I realised, there she was sitting in the front room of a basement flat with a group of strangers, telling us this. With her own parents only a couple of miles away. Who she should have been saying it to, really. And then, of course, she died a few hours later and it occurred to me that you never did hear her say it to you personally. Anyway, that's really the bit I wanted you to know about.

JOE Then why the hell didn't you tell us before now?

KEN I know, I know. That's the terrible thing. We should have done. But at the time, there they were – the press and the television and the police crawling over everywhere – and I said to Kath – let's keep out of it, they never knew about her and us, it's better we keep out of it. So we did. We pretended we hardly knew her. We kept it our secret. Her secret admirers. The only thing is, I could never tell you either, could I? And then, as I say, all these years later I realised that I should have told you, it was very wrong of us not to have told you, that I had to tell you now. To put things right. Only twelve years later, I'm ashamed to. Pathetic.

Pause.

So. Here I am, passing on her love. Better later than never, I suppose.

Another pause.

JOE I think we'll go home, shall we?

KEN Can you try and put it behind you now?

JOE How can I do that? If she loved us as much as you say she did, then why the hell couldn't she come and tell us herself? Instead of taking her own life?

KEN I would advise it. Really I would.

JOE I don't need advice from you, thank you very much.

KEN I'm sorry.

ANDY He's right, Joe. Listen to him –

JOE Look, just go away, both of you, will you? Go downstairs, let yourselves out. Wait in the car, Andy. I'll be down in a minute.

ANDY Are you sure?

JOE I just need a moment to myself *(Getting out his car keys)* Here. *(He throws them to* ANDY*)* Open it up. Don't forget the alarm's on.

ANDY Don't be long.

ANDY *and* KEN *climb over the rope.*

KEN Oh. Warmer again this side.

ANDY Yes.

KEN *(to* JOE*)* I'm sorry – sorry about all that. Good-bye.

JOE *grunts but doesn't look at* KEN. *He is lost in thought.*

ANDY *and* KEN *leave through the arch.*

A silence.

Then, through the door of the room a distant, slightly out of tune piano starts playing a sentimental Victorian ballad.

JOE *sits up and listens incredulously.*

JOE *(softly)* Julia...? Julia...?

He moves slowly towards the door.

(slightly louder) Julia! *(Louder still)* Julia!

ANDY *and* KEN *come hurrying back in.* JOE *is now at the doorway. The piano continues to play.*

(pulling the door fully open and yelling at the top of his voice) JULIA!

The piano playing comes to an interrupted stop in mid-phrase.

The men look at each other.

KEN *(after a pause, cheerfully)* Well. Now she knows we're here.

Blackout.

ACT II

The same.

KEN *(after a pause, cheerfully)* Well. Now she knows we're here.

JOE What was it?

ANDY Is there anyone else in the building?

JOE No. There shouldn't be. No one but us.

ANDY Well, there obviously is.

JOE Who?

ANDY I don't know. Kids. Somebody's broken in. Sneaked in while we weren't looking.

JOE They'd have set something off. The place is full of alarms.

ANDY Didn't you switch it all off just now?

JOE So I did.

Pause.

We'd better take a look, hadn't we?

ANDY Safer to phone the police.

JOE Yes. Well, no. I'm not sure. Maybe.

ANDY You alright?

JOE Yes, I'm fine. I've just had a – it's him – it's his bloody fault – *(Pointing at* **KEN***)* – he got me going for a minute. Imagining Julia was playing the... Bloody ridiculous.

ANDY Forget all that. Right?

JOE Right. Still someone was playing the damn thing. So we'd better find out who. There's three of us. Come on. It'll only be kids.

ANDY and JOE *start to move towards the arch.*

KEN Excuse me.

JOE What?

KEN If it was kids – what piano would they have been playing?

ANDY That's what we're trying to discover. The place is full of pianos. It's a music centre.

KEN I see. Only it sounded to me as if it was coming through that doorway. Only it can't have been. Because the other side of that doorway, as we know, is a solid brick wall.

ANDY Yes, well, occasionally acoustics play strange tricks.

KEN They certainly do.

JOE Look, shall we go and find out? They're probably doing thousands of quids' worth of damage down there. Come on.

JOE *starts to leave again.*

KEN I say...

JOE *(sharply)* What?

KEN I hate to correct you, but it was very definitely coming from that doorway.

ANDY And I'm telling you, it was an acoustic quirk of this building. It can't have done.

KEN It definitely was.

ANDY *(irritated)* It just sounded as if it was.

He strides to the door and opens it.

Look, here. Solid breeze blocks. From floor to ceiling. Wall to wall. Look. It could not have been coming from here. Alright? *(Louder)* Alright?

KEN Steady now.

ANDY So you just keep quiet, alright?

JOE No, he's right, Andy. Just calm down.

Pause.

ANDY Listen. *(Pointing at* **KEN***)* I think this man is somehow having us on. He's got someone else in the building and he's – I don't know why...he's up to something.

KEN I beg your pardon, but what could I possibly be up to? I haven't asked for money. The alternative is that it's a very elaborate practical joke. And I have to tell you I have better things to do with my Sundays than that.

ANDY Maybe you have a grudge.

KEN A grudge?

ANDY Yes, why not?

KEN Against who?

ANDY Against him. Against Mr Lukin.

KEN What are you talking about? I've never met him till today.

ANDY *(in desperation)* Me, then. A grudge against me...

KEN Oh dear, oh dear...

JOE Andy –

ANDY What?

JOE Just shut up a minute. Sit down.

ANDY *(doing so)* I tell you, I am not going along with this. If we start believing all this rubbish there is no guarantee where it will end...

KEN And, with respect, if we don't even consider the possibility of the rubbish being true, we could be in even greater trouble later on.

ANDY Oh, for God's sake...

KEN Now, I've not a great deal of experience in these matters – as I said this isn't my line – but if things run true to form – further things could occur which if we refuse to accept as happening – well, I don't want to put it too strongly – let's just say it could affect your state of mind.

ANDY What the hell are you talking about?

KEN No, listen, no, listen. Just for a minute. Something comes through that door now, say. Say in the shape of Julie. Someone we know to have been dead for twelve years and there she is. Suddenly. Now I'm not saying this will happen, I'm just supposing this. What do we do?

ANDY Run like hell...

KEN Now, no come, on be serious. No, we can do one of two things, can't we? We can look at it, see it and know we're seeing it, so we're getting that message with our eyes to our brain. But when it reaches our brain, if our mind happens to be closed, our brain says to us, no, wrong, it can't possibly be there, have another look. And we look again and we see the same thing and the brain rejects it once more and it happens again, till eventually we get a sort of feedback situation and figuratively speaking we overload and bang go all our circuits. Or. And this is the preferable choice. We look at it calmly and rationally and say, oh hallo, there's a ghost. How very interesting.

ANDY *(sourly)* Have you finished?

KEN I'm just presenting the options, that's all.

JOE Alright. You tell us. According to you, what were we hearing just now? When we heard that piano? I mean, I'm not saying for a minute I believe a single word you're going to say, but what do you think we were hearing?

KEN I think we were hearing Julie.

JOE Julia. Her name's Julia.

KEN Sorry. Julia. We always knew her as Julie, but...

ANDY She hated Julie.

KEN What we heard, surely, was Julia. Playing our old piano.

JOE Your piano?

KEN Yes.

JOE The one that used to be downstairs?

KEN That's right.

JOE When you lived here?

KEN Right.

JOE But it isn't here now, is it?

KEN No, we sold it when we moved.

JOE So she's playing a piano that isn't there?

KEN No, well that's no problem, she's not there either. Not really. But she was, that's the point. And when she was here, so was our piano. And for her it still exists. As does our flat, as do the stairs leading up to that door there, they all still exist. For her. As presumably does the wall between these two rooms. Very simply, the house she's inhabiting is the house that was previously here. Not the one that's here now. That's all.

JOE So why is she here now? What's brought her back?

KEN Well, in my opinion, she probably never left. Sometimes they don't, they hang around. Don't know why. Something, someone, won't let them go. Who knows? Maybe they themselves won't let go. Though I read this article once by a bloke who reckoned, if you died early – suicide, sudden accident, that type of thing – what happens is, you mess up the system – you arrive there wherever it is you go – and they say hey, hang on, you're not due here for another twenty-five years, you'll have to go back and wait your turn. So they leave you here, wandering round. In limbo. Till you are due. Well, it's an interesting theory. I thought it was, anyway.

JOE And why is it we're hearing her all of a sudden? Answer me that.

KEN Yes, I was pondering that. You'd normally need a full seance, at least to be able to hear, say, a piano. No, what we must have created between us, I think, is the equivalent of a seance. I mean, as I say, normally that's the only way you can make a link like this. When there's a number of you all together, concentrating on the same thing. Which of course is what we've been doing. I mean, we've been thinking about Julie – Julia – practically non-stop, haven't we?

JOE Are we likely to hear anything else?

KEN We might. We might well.

JOE From downstairs?

KEN Maybe.

JOE And do you think she'll come up here? I mean, you said she knows we're here? Do you think she'll come up here?

KEN It's a strong possibility. This is all her area, after all. I think this is probably where her presence is going to be strongest. It would make sense.

JOE crosses swiftly to the door and opens it again.

ANDY *(anxiously)* Joe...

JOE listens, then closes the door and stands uncertainly.

KEN She'll be up shortly, I expect, in her own good time.

JOE moves swiftly across to the arch.

JOE I'm going down there. I can't stand this any longer.

ANDY Do you want us to come...?

JOE has gone.

KEN It's alright. He'll be alright. He certainly won't find her down there.

ANDY I hope you appreciate the damage you are doing to that man? The amount of stress he's been under? Since his daughter died? Have you any idea?

KEN I can see he's - not a well man.

ANDY He's never got over his daughter, he loses his wife less than two months ago, yet you put him through this.

KEN I don't think you can blame me entirely –

ANDY What? All these charades, psychic mumbo-jumbo, joke piano playing?

The lights in the room dip.

KEN Well, that's not my doing, anyway.

ANDY No. That is the national grid.

KEN *(consulting his watch)* Oh yes. Everyone switching on for the football probably.

ANDY Don't remind me...

KEN I do have to say one thing to you, though. While he's out of the room. I know you were here. The night she died. I do know you came here, you see.

ANDY *is silent.*

I know at the time you said you didn't. But I was doing the dustbins down in the area there and I saw you coming out of the front door. I mean it wasn't intentional, I just happened to be out there...

ANDY Alright, I was. But that was much earlier in the evening. I wasn't here when she died. I had nothing to do with that.

KEN No, I know you didn't.

Pause.

You do know why she took her life, though, don't you?

ANDY *(quietly)* Yes. Yes, I do.

KEN I thought you might. Of all of us, I thought you would.

ANDY You were right about her mood. That day. It was as if she'd been cured of some dreadful illness. She'd at last come to terms with herself – with real life, her life outside of her music, I mean. Nearly twenty years old and at last she'd managed it. She no longer resented her parents – no longer hated them for all their stifling, misplaced affection. Like a freak in cotton wool – that's how she described herself. Being free of them for eighteen months, hidden away in this little attic – she'd woken up one morning and seen them for what they were. A sad couple full of pride for a child with a talent they couldn't really appreciate or understand. The parents of Little Miss Mozart. And she forgave them – for all the things she felt they'd done to her, because after all they'd only done them with the best will in the world, hadn't they? It's like she told you. She'd learnt to accept love. Instead of resenting it. Treating it as a threat.

Pause.

When I first met her, I used to call her the porcupine. She invited me round for supper – or maybe I invited myself, I forget – and when I got here I stood in that doorway there with this bottle of cheap wine I'd bought. Couple of pizzas. She was sitting there working away as usual and she never even looked up, she just said. Oh, God. You. That's all I need.

KEN *(smiling)* Yes. We used to say to her when she was down with us, now Julie, the only rules here are you must say please and you have to say thank you. And you have to try and smile at least once every five minutes. Otherwise it's liberty hall. *(He laughs)*

ANDY It was ironic. It really was. Over twelve months I'd been coming round here. Five – six nights a week to start with. Sitting with her while she worked, sharpening her pencils, cooking for her – trying to clean up after her – God, she was a tip – weathering all her sarcasm and her put-downs. I just adored her. I used to sit and watch her work for hours. She wasn't even aware of me. And all this beautiful music just pouring out of her. I mean, I used to compose a bit – tried to. I'd slave away for days on end, rewriting, getting it right, bodging it together, trying to make it sound slightly more interesting, original. And in the end it still sounded like everyone else's. It was just so easy for her. Breathtaking. But even so, you know, you can't hold on to your feelings for ever, can you? Not if the other person won't accept them, won't even acknowledge that you have them – If every time you try and touch them, even ever so gently, they practically bite your hand off – well, you tend to lose heart, don't you? After a bit. You think, why am I doing all this? Putting myself through all this misery? I'm not even needed here.

Pause.

Then one day I met Kay. I stayed friends with Julia for a time – Friends? Well, whatever – But on that last night – this was the ironical bit – on that night I was coming round to tell her that I was taking up with Kay and that I probably wouldn't be coming here again – To be honest with you I didn't really think Julia was going to give a stuff one way or the other. But when I arrived, there she was, the minute I came in, standing just there, so excited. Actually waiting. For me. She'd even brushed her hair. Tidied the room. And the worst thing of all – it was the first thing I saw when I came in – she'd made that bed. Clean sheets. God knows where she'd got them. Probably the first time she'd ever done it – looked like a cat's cradle – but anyway, these gleaming white, brand new sheets – *(Indicating the bed)* – like they are there. And I tell you. My heart sank, I don't mind saying.

Pause.

But to give me my due. I didn't slink away and write her a letter – though it did cross my mind. I'd come to tell her I was leaving her and, eventually, I did tell her. When I got a word in edgeways.

Pause.

I don't think she believed me. Not for a long time. She kept saying, no, you don't understand, I love you, you see, I love you. I know now I love you. And I said – I didn't know what to say. She was like a kid. As if that was all going to suddenly change everything. She had no idea. And then she started crying and I told her not to be silly. Then she got angry. And I think I got angry as well. And she started getting really stupid and talking about ending it all and things and that made me really mad because, well, bugger it, I'd put up with a hell of a lot for over a year and she'd never considered my feelings, not once. And she was crying again, kneeling on the floor and hugging herself and saying this was it, this was the last time I'd see her, there was nothing to live for and how could I do this to her –?

Pause.

And anyway I left. I couldn't take any more. I went straight to a party at the other end of town. Can you imagine that, going to a party? Jesus. And I got pissed and slept on someone's sofa. And the next morning, I decided maybe I'd better come back and see how she was.

Pause.

And then I found her.

Silence.

KEN Don't you think you should have told her father all this?

ANDY Joe? That's not the version Joe wants to hear. Come on, you've seen him. That's the version he refuses to face, the one he already knows. Well, maybe not the details, but... Why do you think he's going through all this rigmarole? Bringing me round here? Inviting you? He's looking for another version. From somewhere. It doesn't matter where or what it is. And if it means going through all this psychic, spirit-world business, well, OK. Anything but the real truth – the fact that Julia was completely screwed up since the day she was born by a father who never let her alone for a single second. What sort of truth is that for him to face? For nineteen years that man completely dominated his daughter's life. She told me there wasn't a single second of her childhood when she didn't feel him there, watching her... She was terrified to move on her own. Her only refuge was her music. You saw what she was like, for God's sake. It was as if she'd been born under a rock. And he wonders why she ran away. Why do you think she chose here? She had enough money of her own – even after all the trusts he'd set up which he made sure she couldn't touch – she was still a celebrity – she had some money of her own. But no, she came here. Twelve square feet in some damp little attic. It was about all she could cope with, poor kid. She'd been under that stone so long she couldn't face the daylight.

He pauses.

And to think – I once tried to get her into bed. My God. What must that have done to her?

KEN Well, she seemed to get over that. According to you. Made up that bed of her own free will.

ANDY Too late though, wasn't it?

KEN Yes. I suppose the tragedy of it all, really, is that it was all based on the best will in the world, if you see what I mean. I mean, it was all intended for the best, wasn't it?

ANDY There was a shade of self interest in there somewhere. Just a trace.

KEN Well. Never easy being a parent, is it? Especially daughters. So I'm given to understand. Of course, we only had Alec. I never had that problem. Do you have children, did you say?

ANDY Two.

KEN Any daughters?

ANDY Yes. One. Naomi, yes. But we don't have that problem either. *(Wryly)* Not that one. But then she's a long way short of being a genius at the moment.

KEN Still. It has its blessings, doesn't it? Being ordinary like you and me?

ANDY *(uncertainly)* Yes...

KEN He's been gone a long time, hasn't he? Incidentally...

ANDY What?

KEN Do you happen to know where the sleeping pills came from? The ones she used? I mean, that was always a bit of a mystery, wasn't it? Did you get them for her?

ANDY They belonged to her mother.

KEN Really?

ANDY Julia couldn't sleep. They were prescribed for Dolly. She lent them – gave them to Julia.

KEN That was never mentioned.

ANDY No, well, I think Dolly was too frightened ever to say anything.

KEN What? Frightened of the police, you mean?

ANDY Frightened of Joe.

KEN Ah.

ANDY Besides, I don't think Joe's world includes a wife who needs to take sleeping pills, either. Julia sneaked home on a couple of occasions. Just to see Dolly, apparently. While Joe was away. But don't ever tell him that. It would probably kill him.

KEN No. Of course not.

ANDY Tell me, what do you think? Did he set all this up? The music and so on?

KEN Well, I suppose he could have done.

ANDY Who else?

KEN I must say, that hadn't occurred to me. I just accepted it as a natural phenomenon...

ANDY What? Messages from the spirit world, you mean?

KEN That sort of thing.

ANDY You really do believe it?

KEN Yes, certainly. I've said.

ANDY Truthfully?

KEN Yes.

ANDY That's incredible.

KEN *(concerned)* Oh, dear. You really are at risk, aren't you? Forgive me for asking, but do you believe in a god, by any chance?

ANDY *(with difficulty)* No. Not as a person. Not as an individual in the biblical sense, no. I – think there's – there's probably a life – you know – a life force of – some description – a sort of – cosmic – thing – not sentient – but a cosmic – like a force...like a... *(He gestures vaguely)* I can't say I've given it that much thought, really.

KEN But no afterlife as such?

ANDY Oh, no. Once we're gone we're gone. I believe that.

KEN Therefore no – spirit – no immortal soul, whatever you care to call it?

ANDY Oh, no. Not as individuals, certainly not. No. I don't believe in that.

KEN Ah. How very lonely.

ANDY What are you, then? A fully paid up Christian churchgoer, are you?

KEN No, I'm afraid, far from it. Once a year if I'm lucky. A lot of it's to do with upbringing though, isn't it? I remember talking to my father about this once, you know, the nature of God, religion and so on. I remember he said, ah, well, I can't be a great deal of help to you there, Kenneth. Not on that subject. Which was surprising because on most things he could talk away for hours. He was wonderful like that. He knew about everything. Politics, DIY, VAT, you name it. But he said, no sorry, Kenneth, I'm a bit rocky on that one, son. My only tip to you is this. Whatever you do, try and believe in something or someone greater than yourself. Someone you'll always be able to look up to and live by. Even if it's only the bloke next door. Good advice that.

ANDY Depends where you live.

KEN *(laughing)* Oh, that's good, I like that. Depends where you live. Yes. I must remember that. *(He laughs some more and shakes his head)* So you think Mr Lukin – Joe could have set all this up, do you?

ANDY It's the only explanation. For me, anyway. For a time I thought it might have been you who'd rigged it up for some reason. Maybe for money or for some ulterior reason, I couldn't think what it could be. And then it occurred to me. It might be you and him in it together.

KEN Together?

ANDY Yes.

KEN Why on earth should we do that?

ANDY Well – er – I don't know. For my benefit, I suppose.

KEN For money?

ANDY No. Some reason. Some – I don't know – some ulterior motive.

KEN Another one?

ANDY Yes.

KEN Oh, dear. Full of them, isn't it?

ANDY Well – there has to be one. Doesn't there?

KEN If you say so.

ANDY I do. So. If it isn't you and it isn't you and him, it must be him. Mustn't it? Process of deduction.

KEN Unless it's you.

ANDY Me? How could it be me. Come on. What possible reason could I have?

KEN I don't know, I'm sure. Some ulterior motive, I suppose. *(He laughs)*

ANDY *looks at him suspiciously. He senses a certain mockery.*

ANDY No, it's got to be Joe. It has to. You must see that.

KEN Well. I'm prepared to consider that possibility. I haven't got a closed mind even if some of us have... *(He laughs)* So you reckon he played that music somehow himself?

ANDY He was on his own when it started. We two were just leaving, remember? He asked to be left alone.

KEN Quite right. Possible. There's no way he can have created the atmosphere in here, though. It was overwhelming when I first came in. Well, it was. It's calmer now.

ANDY That is your problem, not mine. Then there were the tapes, of course.

KEN Tapes?

ANDY The ones he played me before you arrived. They're the standard commentary tapes for this room. Part of the guided tour. He managed to - doctor them - somehow. There were traces of what appeared to be her voice recorded over the top of them.

KEN That's interesting. Are they still in the machine?

ANDY Yes. No, hang on, no, they're not. He put back the original tape. At least I think he did. We can soon find out.

ANDY *moves to the red button. As he does so, the lights dip again.*

KEN Is he responsible for that as well, do you think?

ANDY Probably.

KEN Why though? That's the interesting question. Why?

ANDY Who the hell knows. He's lived with this for twelve years. God knows what's going on in his head...

He presses the red button. Nothing happens.

Ah, well...

KEN Nothing?

ANDY *presses the button again.*

ANDY Not a thing. He can't have replaced the original. Unless the thing's just not working any more. Or maybe he's –

KEN Shhh!

ANDY What?

KEN Listen a minute.

ANDY Why, what can you –?

KEN Shh!

After a second, very softly, the sound of a woman crying. It is only just audible.

(in a whisper) Can you hear it?

ANDY *(in a whisper)* What is he playing at now?

KEN *(whispering)* Do you think he recorded this?

ANDY *(whispering)* He has to have done.

JOE *has appeared in the doorway. He listens.*

JOE *(incredulously)* What the hell's going on here?

ANDY *and* KEN *jump slightly.*

The sobbing continues.

What is all this?

JOE I thought you might tell us, Joe.

JOE Eh?

ANDY I just pressed the button, Joe. I didn't record this. This was on there.

JOE What are you talking about?

ANDY The tape. This is what's on your tape.

JOE My tape?

ANDY Yes –

JOE The machine's not even on.

ANDY What?

JOE It's not even on. It's switched off.

ANDY Are you sure?

KEN *(softly)* Well, that is interesting.

Pause. They listen.

The crying stops.

JOE That was Julia.

The others do not reply.

It was, I tell you.

JOE *stares at them both.*

Do you thinking I'm making this up? What do you think I am? Do you think I recorded that myself?

ANDY Well, somebody did.

JOE Just come and have a look. Come on. The whole system is shut down. I switched it off, same time as I did the alarm. Come and see for yourself, if you don't believe me.

ANDY No, I believe you. I'm sorry.

JOE Come on.

ANDY I said, I believe you.

JOE Alright. Well. Thank you so much.

KEN *(to* **ANDY***)* If you don't mind my saying so, you appear to be running out of suspects.

ANDY Then it's somebody else. There's somebody else in this building. Somewhere.

JOE I have been round every room, every broom cupboard. There is no one hiding in here. I can promise you that.

KEN Did you notice the lights dipping at all?

JOE No.

KEN A couple of times?

JOE Can't say I noticed anything.

KEN Must have only been in this part of the house, then. That's interesting.

JOE What does that signify?

KEN Not a lot. Except we seem to be getting a bit of electrical disturbance one way or another.

ANDY And you found nothing? No one?

JOE No. Well – I hesitate to say this because I know you'll laugh at me again but – there are certain areas down there that are definitely colder than others. I mean, I know there's not a lot of heating in the building at the moment, not on a Sunday but – well, there were areas down there where I can tell you it was bloody freezing.

KEN Did they happen to coincide with parts of this original house, do you recall?

JOE Yes, they did. So what happens now? Stalemate, is it? She's down there, we're up here. We can't get to her. What are the alternatives?

ANDY The alternative is to go home, Joe. Back to tea and Mrs Henderson and Kay and the kids. Have a damn good dinner and forget all about this.

KEN That is certainly one alternative.

JOE And the other?

KEN Well –

ANDY There isn't another.

JOE Just a minute. Let him talk...

ANDY Are we going? I'm going.

JOE You know for someone who claims not to believe a word of this, you're more bloody nervous than any of us.

ANDY I'm worrying about you.

JOE Yes, tell you what, I'll worry about me, you worry about you. How about that? Alright? Now let this man speak.

KEN I think the trouble with Andy there is that his options keep narrowing – I think that's the phrase they use, isn't it? My father always said to me, Kenneth, if you insist on being a gambling man, try never to put all your money on the one horse. That way, you may never be a millionaire but at least you won't lose your shirt...

ANDY Your father sounds a right pain in the arse...

KEN *(unoffended)* Oh, he had his moments.

ANDY Wrote to the local paper a lot, did he?

KEN Oh, yes, frequently.

ANDY I thought he would. He sounds the type.

JOE Hey, I say, excuse me... I take it we're still in touch with each other, are we? Still in communication? We were discussing alternatives.

KEN Sorry. Don't know how we got on to that. Yes, well, the other alternative, of course, is to wait and see what happens. See it through.

JOE What do you advise?

ANDY The only choice is to –

JOE (*fiercely*) I'm asking him.

KEN Well, the sensible choice, of course, is to do what Andy suggests and switch off, lock up and all go home.

ANDY Thank you.

KEN However, if we do that, we'll never know, will we? What might or might not have happened. And we'll spend the rest of our lives wondering. So, surely the choice has to be to stay.

ANDY It may be your choice, it's not mine...

JOE Then you'd better go and sit in the car, then, hadn't you? You've still got the car keys...

ANDY OK.

KEN It would be good if you could see your way to staying, Andy.

ANDY Why?

KEN Well, with the three of us – it could just help things along –

JOE Like with the seance?

KEN Exactly. I mean, we don't have to join hands or anything. Feel a bit silly doing that, wouldn't we? But just being here, all of us thinking about her. Might just hurry things along. Help speed up the process.

JOE Andy?

ANDY (*shaking his head*) It's mad. Completely mad.

JOE Bear with us, eh?

ANDY You're not going to get any – sympathetic vibrations. I can tell you that.

JOE Thank you. Ken, you're in charge. What do we do then?

KEN I think if we just – space ourselves round the room.

JOE Sitting down or standing up?

KEN Whichever's most comfortable. She may take her time. But I'm sure she'll be here.

JOE sits on the bed.

KEN sits at the desk.

ANDY, somewhat cussedly, decides to stand by the door.

JOE Andy, you want to sit down?

ANDY No, I'm fine.

A silence.

JOE Well...

KEN Talk if you want to. So long as it's about her.

JOE Right.

Silence.

KEN This her desk, was it?

JOE That's right.

KEN And this'll be some of her music presumably? That she wrote?

JOE No, that's *Greensleeves*. Apparently.

KEN Oh, is it?

JOE According to Andy. Just some music, you know.

KEN Yes. Nice tune, *Greensleeves*.

Silence.

KEN starts whistling Greensleeves under his breath.

ANDY How long do we have to do this?

JOE Till something happens.

ANDY Fine.

Pause.

KEN You were the first one to find her, weren't you?

ANDY What?

KEN That morning. You were the one who first found her, of course.

ANDY I don't want to talk about that, thank you.

Pause.

JOE I never saw her. By the time they'd got hold of me, by the time I got here they'd sealed the room. Taken her away.

Pause.

The hardest part was going home to tell Dolly. I didn't know how she was going to take it. You can't know in advance, can you? Not with things like that. You sometimes imagine how you might react if someone you love – gets taken from you. In your mind, like. But it's never the same when it happens. I mean, in my mind, I was always going to be devastated, you know. Falling apart. Unable to cope. Crying my eyes out. Whereas with Dolly, I assumed it would be the reverse. She'd be the calm one – same as she always was. She'd be the one to cope. But as I say, as it turned out, completely the other way round. I was as calm as could be – well, on the outside anyway – but Dolly – she went completely mad. Like I'd never seen her before in my life. I remember she started attacked me. Hitting, punching, screaming her head off. You bastard. You effing bastard. I mean, she never used language, not Dolly. Unbelievable. Wouldn't let me near her for days. Still, like I say, it takes us all different ways, doesn't it?

Pause.

But I never did see Julia. Here. Never visited. Never got asked. And I was far too proud to come uninvited. Then the only time I did come, on that day, they'd already taken her away. And they wouldn't let me in. Even to sit here.

Pause.

ANDY It was as well you didn't see her.

JOE Where did you find her? Lying near the bed, apparently. Round about here, was it?

ANDY No. The other side. There.

JOE They said there was a lot of blood? Is that right?

ANDY I'm not talking about it.

JOE Why not? Don't you think you owe me that? Andy?

Silence.

ANDY *(softly)* I was at this party. The other side of town. I got really pissed. We'd had a row. Julia and I. *(With a glance at* KEN*)* It doesn't really matter what about. Not any more. But in the morning, I woke up on some sofa and I felt really terrible. Talk about hungover, I think I was still drunk. But the first thought in my head was, I must see if she's OK. Julia. So I thought, I'll go over and see her. I still had my key, you see. I remember walking here, trying to sober up. Lovely sunny morning. It was cold. February. But really bright. And I reached here about nine o'clock. And I let myself into the house and then up the stairs and into this room. The curtains were still drawn and I thought, she's overslept for once, that's unusual, she's usually halfway through a concerto by seven. And I remember standing in the doorway there – getting my eyes used to the darkness – and the first thing I really registered was that bedspread. The last time I'd seen it, it had been white. Only now it wasn't white it was – red. And I thought, oh, Jesus. Oh,

Jesus Christ. What has she done? She can't have done it. Not really. I couldn't see her at first, you see, not from that doorway, she was hidden by the bed. But then as I moved in, I saw... She was... She looked as it she'd lain on the bed for a bit and – I think she must have been in that much pain she – It looked as if she'd tried to get up – maybe for help – but she'd moved away from the door, you see, not towards it – towards that table instead. Maybe she wasn't conscious of where she was any more. Disoriented. But then I think what she was really trying to do was to get back to her music. She'd tried to get back to her music. Only she'd sort of slipped, you see, and was just lying there. They weren't just sleeping pills she'd taken – she'd swallowed every bloody thing she could lay her hands on – she was bleeding from her mouth and her stomach...she must have been in such awful pain and I remember saying, over and over, no, no, no, no, no!

JOE *(softly)* No...

From outside the door, the sound of the piano again. But this time being played discordantly.

Heavy, insistent, rapid, disturbing chords.

The three men freeze.

The chords cease as abruptly as they started.

The sound of a piano lid slamming shut.

ANDY *(in a low whisper)* What's happening? What the hell's happening?

KEN I think she's coming upstairs...

The sound of a distant door closing. Then, on a flight of wooden stairs, a woman's footsteps slowly ascending and approaching.

A pause.

Slowly the door handle starts to move up and down.

The men remain frozen.

WOMAN *(softly, from the other side of the door)* Dad...Dad...
Dad...

The door handle continues to move.

JOE *(softly)* Julia?

ANDY Oh, God...

JOE Let her in. Do you hear me? Let her in. That's my daughter
out there.

The door handle stops moving.

A long silence.

*A sudden heavy pounding on the door, strong enough
to cause the whole door frame to shake.*

As this continues, **JOE** *recovers and steps forward to
grab the door handle.*

ANDY *does likewise.*

They wrestle over the handle.

JOE Let her in! Do you hear me? Let her in!

ANDY *(over this)* You can't let her in. There's no way you're
letting her in here.

KEN *(simultaneously, as he tries to separate them)* You've got
to let her go, don't you understand? You have to release
her, Mr Lukin, it's the only way...

Suddenly the door swings open, violently.

*The breeze block wall has now gone to reveal a shabby,
dimly lit hallway.*

The men are swept aside as if by a violent wind which tears into the room. Books and papers are scattered and blown about. A poster on the wall is violently ripped in half.

The door slams shut.

Silence.

ANDY *and* **KEN** *have apparently been hurled to the ground and now lie at opposite sides of the room.*

But **JOE** *has his eyes fixed on something, someone invisible standing by the bed.*

JOE *(quietly)* Julia... Julia...it's Dad, darling. Julia, look at me. It's Dad.

KEN *(in a whisper)* You have to release her, Mr Lukin... You can't hold on to your daughter any more. Don't you see that? You must see that...

ANDY *(feebly)* Joe, please...

JOE *(appearing not to hear them)* Julia...

JOE *takes a pace or two towards the bed. He holds out his arms, still staring intently at someone only he can see.*

The **WOMAN**'s *voice suddenly fills the room.*

WOMAN *(soft)* ...please...please...please...

JOE *(appalled at what he sees)* Oh, darling...oh my poor, sweet darling... *(With a cry)* Forgive me...!

The **WOMAN**'s *voice stops abruptly.*

Silence.

ANDY *(in horror)* My God, look. Just look at the bed.

Over the white counterpane a red stain is rapidly spreading.

A final long, drawn out scream of pain from the woman fills the room.

JOE *simultaneously drops to his knees.*

Silence.

KEN It's alright now. It's safe now. It's over. *(To* **ANDY***)* You still – in a spot of doubt, are you? Still weighing up the options?

ANDY I don't know – I don't know what – I just don't – I can't... I'm sorry.

JOE *remains on the floor, in a state of shock.*

KEN *moves to him.*

KEN You alright, Mr Lukin? Joe?

JOE *(in a daze)* I saw her, you know. I distinctly saw her. Julia.

KEN *(helping him to his feet)* Yes, I know.

JOE She – looked – so unhappy. So terribly unhappy.

KEN She's not any more, I promise you.

JOE What did I do to her, to make her so unhappy?

KEN *(starting to lead* **JOE** *to the door)* She's happy now, I swear she is. You've released her now, you see. That's all she needed. For you to let her go. Let her rest. There's no need to be frightened. She was just as frightened as we were, you know, most probably. We must have seemed like ghosts to her, you see.

JOE I tried so hard you know, we tried so hard...

KEN *(kindly)* Yes, I know. I know you did. This way now. This way.

JOE *is led gently out by* **KEN**.

ANDY, *following them, cannot resist turning in the arch for a last look at the room.*

ANDY *(softly to himself)* My God!

He shivers and hurries out after the others.

The room is left quiet for a second.

Then, from somewhere, the commentary starts up over the loudspeakers, as at the start.

WOMAN Finally, this is the place where I spent most of my time while I was at college here. The house was then a student residence and this was my room when I was at the university, as a result of winning my music scholarship. It was a considerable change after my home in Otley, West Yorkshire, I can tell you. Quite modest, isn't it? I wonder what Mozart would have made of it...

The voice fades with the lights to a: –.

Blackout.

PROPS

Neatly made bed with a clean white counterpane (p1)
An easy chair (p1)
Bookshelves (p1)
A chest of drawers (p1)
Cupboard etc. (p1)
A small writing table which has some manuscript paper and
pencils rather artistically laid out (p1)
A half-finished mug of 'cocoa' (p1)
Bare boards with the occasional rug (p1)
Rather depressing wallpaper (p1)
One window looking out onto a back alley (p1)
One rather battered teddy bear (p1)
Carpeted section cordoned off by some ornamental rope,
forming a narrow corridor (p1)
Freestanding pedestal fixed to the floor. Mounted on this is
a large red button which, when pressed, operates the pre-
recorded spoken commentary about the room (p2)
Ken attempts to pick up the bear. It is attached to a security
wire, invisible till now, threaded through the counterpane (p37)
Car keys (p48)
Books and papers are scattered and blown about. A poster on
the wall is violently ripped in half (p75)
Over the white counterpane a red stain is rapidly spreading
(p75)

Costume
Andy – he is in his street clothes which suggest that it is a cold
day outside and a not much warmer one inside. Smart but not
expensive clothes. He has made a bit of an effort (p2)

LIGHTING

Blackout (p49)
The lights in the room dip (p56)
The lights dip again (p65)
The voice fades with the lights (p77)
Blackout (p77)

SOUND EFFECTS

Through the overhead speakers a young woman's voice is heard
(p2)
A brief silence on the recording. Then... (p3)
A moment's silence (p3)
The commentary starts up again (p11)
Under the next, on the recording, faintly but quite distinctly, is
the sound of a woman's laughter. It is not a happy laugh (p12)
The recording starts up in mid-sentence (p14)
A brief silence on the recording. Then quite distinctly,
a Woman's voice similar but not the same (in a whisper
increasingly desperate... (p14)
In a whisper (p14)
In a whisper (p14)
In a long drawn out whisper (p14)
A bell rings loudly (p24)
From the outside of the door of the room the sound of footsteps
running down a flight of wooden stairs. They could be a
woman's (p24)
A terrific din as the alarm goes off all around them (p37)
Andy and Ken stand waiting for the din to stop which
eventually it does (p37)
Through the door of the room a distant, slightly out of tune
piano starts, playing a sentimental Victorian ballad (p48)
The piano continues to play (p48)
The piano playing comes to an abrupt stop in mid-phrase (p49)

After a second, very softly, the sound of a woman crying. It is only just audible (p65)

The sobbing continues (p66)

The crying stops (p66)

Ken starts whistling *Greensleeves* under his breath (p70)

From outside the door, the sound of the piano again. But this time being played discordantly (p73)

Heavy insistent, rapid, disturbing chords (p73)

The chords cease as abruptly as they started (p73)

The sound of the piano lid slamming shut (p73)

The sound of a distant door closing (p73)

Then on a flight of wooden steps, a woman's footsteps slowly ascending and approaching (p73)

Slowly the door handle starts to move up and down (p74)

The door handle continues to move (p74)

A sudden heavy pounding on the door, strong enough to cause the whole frame to shake (p74)

The door slams shut (p74)

A woman's voice suddenly fills the room (p75)

The woman's voice stops abruptly (p75)

A final long drawn out scream of pain from the woman fills the room (p76)

Then from somewhere the commentary starts up over the loudspeakers as at the start (p77)

The voice fades with the lights (p77)

VISIT THE SAMUEL FRENCH BOOKSHOP AT THE ROYAL COURT THEATRE

Browse plays and theatre books, get expert advice and enjoy a coffee

Samuel French Bookshop
Royal Court Theatre
Sloane Square
London
SW1W 8AS
020 7565 5024

Shop from thousands of titles on our website

 samuelfrench.co.uk

 samuelfrenchltd

 samuel french uk